PRAYERS UP, WEIGHT DOWN!

A 30-day quest to the best version of you!

CAPRICE O'BRYANT GUTIERREZ

Trailblazer of faith-based weight loss

Prayers Up, Weight Down!
A 30-day quest to the best version of you!

Copyright © 2019 by Caprice O'Bryant Gutierrez

Edited By: Kristie Lacy
Cover inspiration: Kristie Lacy
Cover Designed By: Anna Wilder
Interior Design: Lakia Brandenburg
Cover Photography: Chela Cervantes

Unless otherwise noted all scriptures are from the New Living Translation of the Holy Bible.

ISBN 978-0-692-13725-3

ACKNOWLEDGEMENT

To my Father in Heaven, I thank You for giving me the vision to write and complete this project. I thank You for taking me through the heavy waters and washing me with Your Word, so I can get to know You better. I thank You for helping me destroy my unhealthy habits, so I can teach Your people to do the same. I thank You for still calling on me when I walked in the opposite direction of this book. I thank You, Lord, for the tests and trials that created the testimony and made this book possible. I pray the words I've written brings honor to Your Holy name.

To my Husband,

Thank you for pushing me to grow beyond my fears and excuses to become who God has called me to be! Thank you for inspiring me to be content without ignoring my ambition. I thank you for your love, support and quiet strength!

To everyone who reads,

Thank you for deciding to go on this quest with me! Seven out of ten Americans are overweight, and with God's grace I am determined to make a dent in this rising epidemic. I want to see the Body of Christ healthy and in shape for their calling. I pray this 30-day journey catapults you into a season of winning. I pray that you find like-minded people to support you on this journey; because like our walk with Christ, real lasting change requires community. I hope you re-visit this as often as you need to and get closer to God than you ever have before. I truly hope that your life will be enriched; you will be moved to action and not just inspired. I pray that you will depend on God's grace when will power isn't enough. I pray for a lifetime of wholeness, peace and favor to surround you!

DEDICATION

This book is dedicated to my parents Deon and Vicki, for their sacrifice and hard work to help make my dreams come true.

CONTENTS

INTRODUCTION

I 'm so excited for you! You are dedicating yourself to the strengthening of your mind, body and spirit! Every day there is a scripture from the Holy Bible for you to focus on that keeps your mental and physical health in the forefront of your mind! Your body affects your spirit and soul. It affects how well you function throughout each day. Our bodies and spirits are not one in the same; but as the only vessels for our souls, how we treat and honor the gifts that God has given us is vitally important.

Before I was obedient to God about taking care of my body, I kept everything separate. I did that only because I wasn't aware of the power that they had together. Understanding that they are both quite emotional journeys led me to making sure I kept God in literally *all* that I do.

Some may think that combining your faith and fitness is as simple as asking God for strength during a plank when it feels like your body is collapsing. While it is true that I will certainly call on Jesus when I'm already shaking 9 seconds into a one-minute plank, I'm ready to take you on a deeper journey. Faith, fitness, nutrition and accountability are the essential tools to making Prayers Up, Weight Down an effective and lasting lifestyle!

For the next 30 days I am going to take you on a quest. You'll read the scriptures that helped me love the body God gave me while improving it at the same time. You'll try some of my favorite healthy recipes that keep my body strong. You'll learn how to take authority over your mind so that you rebuke the lies of the enemy and stand on the truth of what God says about you! You'll experience my workouts that release so many endorphins that you feel like a million bucks. We're going to send prayers up, and the weight is going to come down. Are you ready?

DAY ONE
SURRENDER

"Surrender yourself to the Lord and wait patiently for Him."

PSALM 37:7

I was chatting with a former client one day about weight loss —let's just call her Molly. Molly was down about her body. She had this nagging feeling about "letting herself go". Even her posture showed her disappointment! My advice to her was to pray about it and write down what she could do to turn it around. She already felt a certain way about the little girl who's never been overweight a day in her life telling her what to do, and then I was telling her to pray? With a disturbed look she said, "Caprice, if I pray to God about my body all He's going to say is lose weight." I'm pretty sure we laughed for 5 minutes straight. Forcing myself to get it together, I challenged her with a different perspective.

As it was, she felt that her weight was the problem and losing weight was the solution. Hesitantly I asked her, what led to you (I air quoted), "letting yourself go?" She began telling me about her relational struggles and how things used to be different when her lifestyle was more stable. Weight wasn't an issue she said, "I was comfortable with my body." She expressed that she was trying to fill a void and food was the drug of choice. Something I know most of us can relate to. I reassured her that the way she felt was real and she didn't deserve to be hurt, but the only one that could successfully fill that void is God. If Molly prayed about being tired of struggling to get the weight off, she'd find that it's not just the physical weight she needs to get rid of. It's also the hurt and rejection from the abusive relationship that she didn't heal from. It's the habits and choices that caused the pounds to add up.

These kinds of strongholds can weigh us down quickly, mentally and physically, but we have power over them!

To my friends reading this, the weight of your past, present or future does not belong on your shoulders. That burden leads to stress, and do you know what happens to our bodies when we are stressed? Our bodies release a hormone called cortisol and its job is to tell your body to store fat.

Right now, I need YOU to surrender the burdens with your body and mental wellness to God. His yolk is easy, and His burden is LIGHT! Give it all to God, He can handle it. On the contrary, don't try to skip the struggle, because *great things take time*. If you are struggling to pinpoint what is weighing you down, then it's time to pray for God to reveal that to you. You cannot heal what you do not confront!

Pray with me: "God, I am not pleased with my body, but I want to be. I am no longer going to let the stress in my life keep me from achieving my goals. I just want to give it all to You! I cannot do it by myself. Thank You for guiding me on the path that I am to take to total health and wellness. Thank You for giving me all the tools and resources I need to be successful. Thank You for showing me areas where I need to begin healing. Lord, You are good! Thank you. In Jesus' name, Amen."

REFLECT

What has been revealed to you that is weighing you down? Also, write down the specific goal that you are surrendering to the Lord. How much weight do you need/want to lose?

_____

_____

_____

_____

_____

_____

_____

_____

_____

_____

_____

_____

_____

_____

_____

_____

_____

TODAY'S WORKOUT

WARM UP
20 sec light jog; 20 sec fast high knee; 30 sec jumping jacks. X2
*Following the warm up, repeat leg circuit in order
with minimal rest in between exercises.

EXERCISE	REPS
Squat w/Glute kick backs	12 reps each leg
Good mornings	12 reps
Standing side leg lifts	15 each side
Bridges	15 reps
Inner thigh leg lifts	15 each side
Wall sit	45 sec

Perform circuit for 3 rounds.
Aim to only rest in between the whole round.
Rest for 1-2 minutes between circuits.
Stretch well once complete.

DAY TWO
OF COURSE, IT'S POSSIBLE

Jesus looked at them and said, "with man this is impossible,
but not with God; All things are possible with God."

MARK 10:27

The same way you apply the unfailing promises of God to your finances, and tough circumstances, apply it to your health and wellness goals. Regardless of what anyone has said to you about what's possible with your body and what's not, choose to speak life over yourself.

When you live a sedentary lifestyle and consume more carbs than you burn, it can lead to elevated blood sugar and increased abdominal fat. But when you start exercising and getting rid of the extra weight you are carrying, you can reverse insulin resistance before it gets to type 2 diabetes! Even if you have reached the point of diagnosis, it is still not over! Did you know that FOOD IS MEDICINE? It *is* possible to reverse the effects of type 2 diabetes. You, first, must believe it before you can see it. You must understand that just like EVERY other promise, EVERY other time you needed God He was there and this is no different. Read Mark 11:24, "I tell you, you can pray for anything and if you believe you've received it, it will be yours."

Second, it is important to educate ourselves! Type 2 diabetes impacts how our bodies metabolize glucose; we either resist insulin or don't produce enough insulin! Insulin regulates the movement of glucose in our cells while glucose is our body's main source of energy. We get glucose from food. When you consume foods that are constantly increasing your blood sugar, the sugar just builds up in your bloodstream and your body can't make enough insulin to keep up. Foods like cereal, bagels, breads, fried foods, candy, dairy, etc. are examples of food that increase your blood sugar. To success-fully reverse diabetes, you need to eat foods that take longer to be digested and metabolized so they don't cause a sudden spike in your blood glucose and insulin levels. Eat more fiber: berries, nuts, seeds, asparagus, green beans and all veggies! You want your plate to be bright and colorful. You don't need to over complicate it. The more fatty tissue you have, the more you are at risk for type 2 Diabetes. Let's get moving and **"Let the grocery store be God's pharmacy!"** –**Peggy Riggins.** Broccoli can help improve your glucose tolerance. Beets are proven to reduce inflammation. Turmeric is known for its strong anti-oxidant properties. Parsley can keep your immune system strong and flush excess fluid from your body. Take a deep breath. You can do this. I believe in you! Now go to the mirror and repeat, "I believe in myself".

Pray with me: "Father God, today I choose to believe your report that victory belongs to me in Jesus! The world wants me to believe that my goals are unattainable and unrealistic! But I declare and decree that a healthy body is mine if I am willing to fight for it. Lord Thank You for the strength to run with endurance away from the unhealthy habits of my past. Thank You for giving me a fresh vision of the strong, healthy body that is on the other side of fear and limit-ing beliefs. Thank You for this opportunity to grow! I recognize that I have extraordinary abilities because I belong to Jesus and I receive them today and every day by faith! Thank You. In Jesus' name, Amen."

REFLECT

Whether you want to release 10lbs or 100lbs, do you truly believe that you can lose it and keep it off? If you are struggling to believe it is even possible use the space below to write out what is hindering your faith, then repeat aloud Mark 10:27 and memorize it.

_____

_____

_____

_____

_____

_____

_____

_____

_____

_____

_____

_____

_____

_____

_____

_____

TODAY'S WORKOUT

WARM UP

20 sec ice skaters; 20 sec butt kicks; 30 sec jumping jacks. X2
*Following the warm up, repeat circuits in order for
2-3 rounds each. Stretch well once complete.

EXERCISE	REPS/TIME	REST
1ST CIRCUIT		
Jackknives	12 reps	
Cross mountain climbers	20 reps	Rest 1 minute
Oblique reaches	20 reps	
Star jumps	12 reps	
2ND CIRCUIT		
Leg raises	30 reps	
X Crunches	20 reps	Rest 1 minute
Plank	30 sec	
Squat jumps	15 reps	

DAY THREE
SELF-LOVE

"You shall love your neighbor as yourself."

MARK 12:31

G od's love is a gift that we release to others through our actions and words, but sometimes we only show love to others and neglect ourselves. Choosing not to love ourselves is just as bad as choosing not to love others. God longs for us to love ourselves and our identity in Him.

Joyce Meyer says, "You cannot give away what you don't have!" This is another way of saying "you can't pour from an empty cup." Often, we pour out so much love to others that we end up depleting ourselves. Why should we constantly show up second place in our lives? I remember attending an event that changed my own perspective on self-love. The speaker asked us to write down who and what we loved. After everyone was finished with their list she asked, "Where is your name on that list?" Wow. My name was nowhere on the list. That was such a stark revelation to me! To be transparent, it still took me a *long* time to apply what was revealed on that day. It took for many things to fall apart in my life before I recognized that *I* needed to be the one in first place! My interests and my health shouldn't keep taking a back seat. The same goes for you! Aside from loving God, self-love is the greatest, sweetest love of all!

Don't feel bad about choosing an exercise class over having dinner with a friend because self-love is not selfish or arrogant. Self-love is to accept you fully: the darkness, the light, the good, the bad and ugly. Self-love is extending the grace to yourself that God gives to you. Literally everything you do in life starts with your physical well-being. The only way to consistently show up as your authentic self is to be sure there are no interfering physical or mental barriers like poor health, pain, fatigue or bad attitude. The way you can be proactive about this is to intentionally take care of your body and guard your mind. You must be kind to your body. You shouldn't abuse or neglect it. You must feed your mind with the word of God. You have to stay in good shape as a whole: physically, mentally and spiritually.

Now is the time to draw near to God and receive His love so you can begin to pour it out to yourself—first. Self-love is a pre-requisite to loving other people. If you want your relationships to thrive you must love yourself before you attempt to love anyone else. *Self-love is an ever-lasting appreciation for yourself!*

Pray with me: "Lord I thank you for your endless and unfailing love! I ask that you show me how to love and appreciate all that I am and all that I'm not. Teach me how to create healthy boundaries, teach me how to forgive myself, teach me how to protect my heart, teach me how to practice self-care intentionally. Help me to be kind to my body. Lord, please convict me when I am not operating in self-love.

In Jesus' name, Amen"

REFLECT

Write down what you love about yourself. Then write down any habits and conscious behaviors that prove to be opposite of loving yourself.

_____

_____

_____

_____

_____

_____

_____

_____

_____

_____

_____

_____

_____

_____

_____

_____

_____

TODAY'S WORKOUT

WARM UP
20 sec light jog; 20 sec fast high knee; 30 sec plank jacks.
*Following the warm up, repeat arm circuit in order
with minimal rest in between exercises. (20-30 sec)

EXERCISE	REPS
Mountain Climbers	30 sec
Tricep Dips	12 reps
Inch worm	12 reps
Superman	15 reps
Arm circles	60 sec

Perform circuit for 3 rounds.
Rest for 1-2 minutes between circuits.
Stretch well once complete.

DAY FOUR
OPERATING IN PEACE

'Only God gives inward peace, and I depend on him. God alone is the mighty rock that keeps me safe and he is the fortress where I feel secure."

PSALM 62:5-6

O nce we receive Jesus—the Prince of Peace—we can acquire inner peace.

Inner peace is a wholeness of your mind and spirit where you can experience total rest. Jesus slept in the storm. He was completely unbothered. Read Matthew 8:23-27. God wants that for you! He wants you to experience the peace that surpasses all understanding. That type of peace allows you to know what contentment feels like. When you are content you are proud of where you are while you are working towards what's next. We tend to believe that once our circumstances change or our environment becomes different we will feel peace. But Jesus said, "peace I leave with you, peace I give to you; I do not give as the world gives." Peace doesn't depend on others. Peace doesn't depend on if we have a flat stomach or not. Peace is a fruit of the spirit. You can have peace during adversity. You can be at peace with your body while transformation is under way. When we learn to live in peace with ourselves and others, we spend less time stressing over the scale and envying our friends if they lose weight quicker than us. But we make so many decisions everyday. What to eat, what to wear, what street to turn down, etc. These decisions impact our physical, spiritual and emotional health and definitely our peace!

Today just know that forward is forward. Stay the course, but stay in peace! Because what good is a six pack if you carried the weight of your past with you in your heart? Then you are still in bondage! Your chains can keep you stuck. Have you ever moved to a new city to start fresh but nothing changed? Was there no peace? Let's consider the Israelites. The Word says God led them out of Egypt, "But my people would not listen to me. They kept doing whatever they wanted, following the stubborn desires of their evil hearts. They went back instead of forward." —Jeremiah 7:24. You need peace and wholeness, my friend.

Pray with me: "Lord thank you for this inner peace that I have been searching for. I thank you for placing calmness in my spirit. Sometimes the battlefield in my mind is too much to bear. Thank you for reminding me that peace does not mean perfection! Thank you for allowing me to practice peace today and helping me to build my peace muscles. I trust your love, God, and I surrender it all to you! In Jesus' name, Amen"

REFLECT

What do you not feel at peace about in terms of your physical and mental well-being?

_____

_____

_____

_____

_____

_____

_____

_____

_____

_____

_____

_____

_____

_____

_____

_____

_____

TODAY'S WORKOUT

WARM UP

20 sec light jog; 20 sec fast high knee; 30 sec jumping jacks.
*Following the warm up, repeat circuit in order
with minimal rest in between exercises.

EXERCISE	REPS
Russian Twists	30 reps
Scissor Kicks	30 reps
Alternating side lunges	35 sec
Push up plank	45 sec
Burpees	12 reps
Wall sit	45 sec

Perform circuit for 3 rounds.
Rest for 1-2 minutes between circuits.
Stretch well once complete.

DAY FIVE
CONQUERING TEMPTATION

"No test or temptation that comes your way is beyond the course of what others have had to face. All you need to remember is that God will never let you down; he'll never let you be pushed past your limit; he'll always be there to help you come through it."

1 CORINTHIANS 10:13

God gives us extremely powerful points of encouragement in this verse! Fitness journeys can be so emotional. Most things are different than anything we have ever experienced. We try different foods. Our bodies move in different ways. It can be a test of our determination, will power and focus! What God is telling you right now is that you are not alone. You aren't the first person to lose your way and become unsatisfied with your body. You aren't the first person to hate eating spinach and doing burpees. Want to know what is great? God is just waiting for you to tell him how it is tough for you – He already knows the way out. "I know how to help you endure this difficult task! I have helped them, and I will help you too."

For years you could have been drinking Dunkin Donuts coffee every day, eating fried chicken every Tuesday, and the list could go on. Having to reverse those bad habits can seem overwhelming or even impossible. It can seem like you've reached the end of your rope and you won't be able to break those routines, but just tie a knot and hang on! Be proud of yourself. You could be doing nothing and just accepting defeat, obesity or poor health. Instead, you are striving to become the best version of you. You are preparing for God to do a new thing in you! Stay the course. It is not easy, but it will literally make you stronger: physically and spiritually. Physically you are exercising and building muscle for a strong body. To develop a strong spirit, you must also feed it a healthy diet. This diet will consist of reading the Word every day to strengthen the muscles and increase the endurance of your spirit! Having a strong spirit allows you to overcome temptation and take authority over your flesh and its desires. Reading the Bible every day allows the Word of God to wash you and cleanse you from what you once were. If you only take a shower every couple of days, you won't stay clean. In the same way, if you only pick up the Bible every couple of days, you won't keep a strong spirit. Remember that you are not alone. You are going to inspire so many people just because you didn't give up!

Pray with me: "Lord I thank You for being a forgiving God. I thank You for teaching me how to fight temptation and overcome my unhealthy habits. I thank You for being the God of my success and the God of my mistakes! Thank You for changing me from the inside out. I don't want to hang on to the old things of the past, Lord. I know the enemy wants me to be condemned and discouraged for falling off, but Your Word says that sin no longer has dominion over me! Thank You for restoration today! In Jesus' name, Amen."

REFLECT

What temptations are you currently struggling to overcome? In what situations are you more likely to succumb to temptation?

_____

_____

_____

_____

_____

_____

_____

_____

_____

_____

_____

_____

_____

_____

_____

_____

_____

_____

_____

_____

TODAY'S WORKOUT

Rest your body!
Foam roll. Go for a walk if you wish.
Stretch for at least 20 minutes!

DAY SIX
CARING FOR YOUR BODY

"No one hates his own body but feeds and cares for it, just as Christ cares for the church."

EPHESIANS 5:29

The time is now. You need to feed and care for your body. Keep reaching toward new habits, because the foods you choose to eat determine how well your body functions. Sometimes I feel lousy and like I need soul food, something greasy; maybe baked macaroni with steak or an Italian beef sandwich with mozzarella cheese and peppers. I feel like I've worked hard so this is what I deserve, but deep down I know the consequences of putting those things into my body.

What I really need to do is focus on feeding my spirit and not my soul. You have a spirit and you have a soul. According to Carl McLeod, "Your spirit is the superior part of your inner person and your soul is the lower part." With your spirit you can receive God and have faith. Within your soul, you house human emotion, feelings, desires and aversions. Soul food exhausts you and food for your spirit energizes you. Only feeding your soul will cause you to operate in your flesh.

I do my best not to choose temporary satisfaction. It interrupts my digestive system; it makes me feel lazy, drained, and lethargic! Can you relate? Because it is what I want at the time, I allow my feelings to justify my choice. As delicious as they can be, certain foods are a heart attack waiting to happen. I constantly remind myself of the responsibility I have to protect and care for my body. This is huge! **God is TRUSTING *me* with my body.** Wow. Christ will do anything for the church, His Body, so why are we so reluctant to do anything for our bodies? Moment of truth – you only get one. So, what are you going to do to nurture it?

Knowing what triggers you is important. Once you know what your triggers are, you can become successful in delaying instant gratification and emotional eating. Temporary feelings of euphoria can cause you to make poor decisions. For example, knowing that big meetings or tests make you want to drink an entire bottle of wine or eat 2 large pizzas, gives you power over those cravings. The enemy doesn't have any new tricks. He will use the same things to trip you up time and time again to distract you from what God needs you to do!

I want you to ask God to reveal you, to you. Coming face to face with your flaws and bad habits is an opportunity to grow! When you ask God to put a magnifying glass on **you,** you give Him permission to sharpen you. Let's dig deeper into why you immediately resort to binging. Think about what makes YOU tick, stare it in the face and deal with it. Unhealthy habits are formed when you feel an emotion and choose to act on it, without regard to what's causing it. **Next time you experience those emotions, submit them to God. Consider this: you may be hungry for something that chocolate cannot provide. So, give yourself 15-20 minutes before you unwrap the Twix.**

Pray with me: "Father God, I thank You for loving me past my imperfections. I want to be sharpened, Lord. I know sometimes it may be uncomfortable and it may not be easy. I ask that You reveal the triggers that cause me to fall short of my goals and excellence.

Heighten my discernment so that I can recognize Your tests and pass them. I want to be a stronger vessel in the Body of Christ, but I need Your wisdom. Thank You for searching me, O God. I wait in great expectation. In Jesus' name, Amen."

REFLECT

What emotion led you to overindulge last time? What feeling came before you decided to eat unhealthy foods?

_____

_____

_____

_____

_____

_____

_____

_____

_____

_____

_____

_____

_____

_____

_____

_____

_____

TODAY'S WORKOUT

WARM UP

5 min treadmill or 150 jump rope

*Following the warm up, repeat each circuit in order with minimal rest in between exercises for 2-3 rounds.

Stretch well once complete.

EXERCISE	REPS/TIME	REST
1ST CIRCUIT		
Bird dog	60 sec	Rest 1 minute
Flutter Kicks	30 reps	
Reverse crunches	20 reps	
Butterfly crunches	25 reps	
Jumping jacks	50 reps	
High knees	40 sec	
2ND CIRCUIT		
Mountain climbers	10 sec	
Push up	1 rep	
Plank	10 sec × 8	

DAY SEVEN
PATIENCE IN THE PROCESS

"But if we hope for what we do not see, we wait for it with patience."

ROMANS 8:25

P atience was the hardest part of my journey because it wasn't natural. I had to learn that patience teaches you to endure without complaining. It teaches you how to wait with a smile. When I was still having frequent seizures, people used to tell me to be patient and I would see God's work revealed. That was the absolute last thing I wanted to hear.

I started praying to God to be completely healed from seizures, when before I would pray to accept what I cannot change. It was so difficult to imagine myself seizure free because it was such a huge part of who I was. I was "the waitress with seizures" and then "the trainer with seizures". I had to believe bigger. I prayed big and bold prayers and got to work. I started taking care of myself intentionally. I swapped Mucho Mango for water. I swapped flaming hots for Skinny Pop popcorn and kale chips. I swapped mashed potatoes with milk and butter for sweet potatoes with cinnamon. I made wise choices and remained faithful and patient through the process of healing.

I chose not to be stagnant in my waiting season. I desired to be still and honor God for who He was and the work He was doing in my life! Only, God told me to be still, not stand still. Standing still is sitting around waiting for God to snap his fingers to change your situation. But being still and knowing that HE is God is actively preparing for what it is that you are praying for. You aren't moving ahead of God and trying to accomplish things in your flesh, but you aren't sitting on your hands not doing anything either. Miracles happen in movement. Be still in your heart and mind while you move by faith.

You can do this. But you don't have to do it alone. I have your back, and most importantly God does. He will never fail you. Keep the hope in your heart that you will get off your medication; that you will play in the yard with your grandkids one day; that you will do yoga in the park and that you will become the great person that God has called you to be. Stay hopeful, patient and pray without ceasing. I declare a shameless persistence over you! You will not grow weary. This journey is making you stronger than you thought was possible!

Pray with me: "Father God, I know that only true health comes from You. I know that if I stay the course I will succeed, but it is easy for me to get discouraged about how far I must go on this journey. I invite You into this health and fitness journey God! Interrupt me when I am spending time on things that will not push me towards my goals. I invite You to teach me to have the patience I need. Lord, help me gravitate towards foods that do my mind and spirit good and not harm. I have not been able to sustain this on my own, but I know I am accomplishing it now by the power of your spirit, God! Today I put on the garment of self-control and walk in the confidence in which you created me to have. Thank You, Lord. In Jesus' name, Amen."

REFLECT

Do you get impatient with weight loss and look to commercial remedies to get the weight off quicker?

TODAY'S WORKOUT

WARM UP

Dynamic stretching, light 5-minute jog

*Following the warm up,

repeat leg circuit in order for 2-3 rounds.

Stretch well once complete.

EXERCISE	REPS/TIME	REST
Squat w/knee up crunch	35 sec	
Star jumps	20 sec	
Donkey kicks	25 each leg	
Fire hydrant	20 each leg	Aim to only
Straight leg pulse	20 each leg	rest in between
Squat jumps	30 sec	entire circuit
Lunges	15 each leg	
Deadlifts	12 reps	
Squat pulse	35 sec	

DAY EIGHT
REST MATTERS

"Remember the Sabbath day, to keep it holy. Six days you shall labor, and do all your work, but the seventh day is a Sabbath to the LORD your God. On it you shall not do any work."

EXODUS 20:8–11

REST is a part of the program! I've had plenty of clients that were super eager to reach their goals. That's great except they would work too hard in the beginning and burnout. You don't need to work out 7 days a week, 2 hours a day. Slow down a bit. It is amazing that you are fired up, but you are breaking down muscle fibers when you exercise. We need muscle to burn fat but if you are constantly tearing the muscle and not allowing time for it to heal you are doing your body no good! The only way to get stronger is to recover. You must also let your mind rest. When learning how to eat clean and change your body composition, you're constantly learning. There is tons of information being thrown at you, some valuable—some not. I'm sure you have seen people saying things like, "no days off". <u>Wrong!</u> You need days off. I usually rest on Wednesdays and Sundays. You cannot pour from an empty cup. Recharge your batteries. Reflect on how far you've come and just relax!

Here are a few successful rules to live by.

1. Never miss a Monday workout.
2. Never go 3 days in a row without exercise.
3. Don't over train your muscles. (Example: doing the same exercise everyday)
4. Listen to your body.

Pray with me: "Lord, thank You for my life! Thank You for giving me permission to rest my mind and body. Often it is hard for me to do this on my own or without situations forcing me to. The world moves so fast and I constantly feel as though I need to keep up by hustling. I relinquish the control I think I have over my life and surrender it all to You! I will rejoice in the new strength I will receive from this rest. Thank You, Lord! In Jesus' name, Amen."

REFLECT

Do you trust God enough to rest? What does this mean to you?

_____

_____

_____

_____

_____

_____

_____

_____

_____

_____

_____

_____

_____

_____

_____

_____

_____

_____

TODAY'S WORKOUT

Rest your body!
Foam roll. Go for a walk if you wish.
Stretch for at least 20 minutes!

CONTROLLING YOUR THOUGHTS

"Be careful how you think. Your life is shaped by your thoughts."

PROVERBS 4:23

To truly evolve into the man or woman that you are destined to be, you must be in control of your thoughts. Negative thoughts can cause intense anxiety, sickness and disease. We are all working to win the battle in our mind. Your thoughts become words and words have power! If you constantly think and repeat, "I'm never going to lose this weight", "nothing is going to help me", and "I hate my body" there will be nothing positive to come. The word of God tells us that "our words have the power to destroy and the power to build up." Refer to Proverbs 12:6. Are your words destroying or building up? God gives us the authority to speak to our problems. We are called to speak to our weaknesses. Speak the word of God over them.

When you pay attention to your thoughts, you will notice how they can take you captive. The lies of the enemy can creep in and make you feel like a prisoner in your own mind. The enemy will attempt to condemn you, cripple you with fear, paralyze you with anxiety and make you feel like hiding. What's the point of going back to the gym if I'm going to quit again next week? Why should I keep buying vegetables if I'm going to waste them? I don't finish anything. If only I was shaped like her. If only I could do pull-ups like him. NEVER be afraid to say: "Leave me alone! Not today Satan!" Those are all lies of the enemy to distract you and keep you bound. When you resist the devil, he will flee from you. The devil is an opposer. He doesn't want you to get your house in order. He doesn't want you organized and disciplined. He wants to stop every good thing the Lord is doing in you. We must replace that condemnation and those lies with the truth found in God's Word. We fight back with scripture. Jesus always fought the enemy by using the Word as a sword. That is how we learn to take our thoughts captive. Negative thoughts can be very debilitating, but let's continue learning how to mute the lies of the enemy.

To be successful, we replace the lies with the truth!

1. **Fight against fear.**
    God created you to thrive not survive. You cannot thrive living in fear.

    "For God has not given us the spirit of fear and timidity, but of power, love and self-discipline."
    2 TIMOTHY 1:7

2. **Fight against condemnation.**
    Your redeemer lives! He knows you are a sinner and may fall short, but He loves you anyway. Being convicted by God is to be under His discipline, which is an honor!

"But the Lord will redeem those who serve him. No one who takes refuge in him will be condemned."

PSALMS 34:22

3. **Fight against impatience.**
   When we acknowledge Jesus in our lives we desire to be more like him. When he left the physical world, he promised us a helper to be with us always, the Holy Spirit. Let's be doers of the word and take on the fruits of the spirit! Impatience comes from our flesh desiring to have answers right away, quick fixes, etc.

   *"But the Holy Spirit produces this kind of fruit in our lives: love, joy, peace, **patience,** kindness, goodness, faithfulness, gentleness, and self-control."*

   GALATIANS 5:22

4. **Fight against comparison.**
   We can never compare our journey to someone else's because we don't have the same starting point. And it is a fact that you will never get strong watching someone else lift.

   "Pay careful attention to your own work, for then you will get satisfaction of a job well done, and you won't need to compare yourself to anyone else. For we are each responsible for our own conduct."

   GALATIANS 6:4–5

5. **Fight against feeling worthless.**
   God created you for a high purpose! Every single day of your life has been planned. God chose you!

"For I know the plans I have for you, declares the Lord, plans for good and not for evil, to give you a future and a hope!"

JEREMIAH 29:11

Pray with me: "Lord, I denounce thoughts of fear, defeat, anxiety, and agitation! I declare that I am adopting thoughts of happiness, grace, favor and blessings! I will meditate and concentrate on truth and goodness. Father, You know my thoughts whether good or bad. From this day forward may my thoughts and words be pleasing to you, God! I thank You for placing a hedge of protection around my mind so that my thoughts may be pure. When evil or negative thoughts begin to trample me, I ask for your strength to rebuke them at their onset! I will diligently guard my mind so that unhealthy thoughts will no longer control me! In Jesus' name, Amen."

REFLECT

Take your time and write down the thoughts that have been sab-
otaging your goals. Be sure to write and declare the truth from
God's Word after writing the lie of the enemy.

_____

_____

_____

_____

_____

_____

_____

_____

_____

_____

_____

_____

_____

_____

_____

_____

_____

_____

_____

_____

TODAY'S WORKOUT

WARM UP

Dynamic stretching, 150 jumping jacks or 150 jump rope
*Following the warm up, repeat circuit in order.

EXERCISE	REPS
High knees	30 sec
Forearm Plank	60 sec
Burpees	30 sec
Coffin sit ups	60 sec
Jumping jacks	30 sec
Reverse Crunches	60 sec

Perform circuit for 3-4 rounds.

Rest for 20-30 sec between exercises. Rest for 1-2 minutes between rounds. Stretch well once complete.

DAY TEN
WALK WITH COURAGE

"Be strong and courageous. Do not fear or be in dread of them, for it is the LORD your God who goes with you. He will not leave you or forsake you."

DEUTERONOMY 31:6

The courage God gave Solomon to rule a kingdom is available to you! Fix your posture right now because we are called to be determined and confident. Be determined enough not to quit when things become challenging. We must do the work. God is not a genie. It seems like as adults we are always on the go and we put ourselves on the back burner too easily. Don't become so obsessed with being busy that you place your confidence in worldly things. Be confident in who you are in Christ. He wants to fight your battles, but while we know God is working in the spiritual, that does not give us the right to be lazy in the physical. When you are about to pull out an excuse say: "Nope! Just do it." You cannot advance if you don't move. Be determined when everything feels like it's falling apart. Be determined when others would understand if you quit. Be determined. Be confident. God is with you!

Pray with me: "Lord, I thank You for new grace today. I thank You for protecting my heart, mind and spirit! I thank you for giving me determination and favor to keep going on this journey. Impart to me the spirit of joy so that I can keep going in hope, without complaining. Empower me to seek You consistently in prayer when I feel stagnant or weak. Empower me to have a determination to complete the tasks set before me. I ask for courage Lord. I know that if I want something to change, I must change something. Thank You in advance for the courage and tenacity to carry that truth out! In Jesus' name, Amen."

REFLECT

What do you believe God is saying to you today?

_____

_____

_____

_____

_____

_____

_____

_____

_____

_____

_____

_____

_____

_____

_____

_____

_____

_____

_____

_____

_____

TODAY'S WORKOUT

WARM UP

30 sec standing oblique crunches;
20 sec fast high knee; 30 sec plank jacks. X2
*Following the warm up, repeat arm circuit in order.
Stretch well once complete.

EXERCISE	REPS
Shoulder taps	30 sec
Tricep dips	15 reps
Tricep push ups	15 reps
Plank walk ups	30 sec
Superman with reach	15 each side
Side planks	30 sec each side

Perform circuit for 3 rounds.
Rest for 1-2 minutes between each.

DAY ELEVEN
DON'T CONFORM

"Don't copy the behavior and customs of this world, but let God transform you into a new person by changing the way you think. Then you will learn to know God's will for you, which is good and pleasing and perfect."

ROMANS 12:2

As women and men of faith we are not to copy the trends and fashions of this earthly world but allow God's presence to bring us to an understanding of His will. To transform your body, you must transform your mind. Period. There is no way around it. So you have to guard your mind! Because of course, in America there is a fast food restaurant on just about every corner. Their signs scream familiarity and convenience, but we still buy into it and the heart attacks they can cause.

Lots of things motivate and inspire us but for lasting change to occur, action must be taken. The Word tells us, "don't copy" or in other translations "do not conform." That is a call to ACTION! Change your mind, change your life. *But how?* There must be a conscious shift. We start by identifying how we think about ourselves, how we think about food and exercise. On day nine we talked about how important our thoughts are, but we are going deeper today. This is a process. God keeps every single answer we seek right in His word. Ephesians 4:23 says, "Instead, let the spirit renew your thoughts and attitude." Speak that over your life, receive it and it is so! Notice how we are asking God to let the spirit renew our thoughts, not our flesh. So, when it gets challenging repeat, "renew my mind Lord", because it's not your spirit that wants a double cheeseburger, it's your flesh. Just because everyone else around you has lived with poor habits for years does not mean you have to keep them going. Break the mold! I believe in you. Keep going!

Pray with me: "Lord I stand in awe of Your mercy today! I praise You for making me new and seeing every wonderful thing about me when the world pushes me to the side. Transform my mind God! Thank You for reminding me that Your plans are perfect, and Your ways are better. God, I pray that my obedience will further your Kingdom. I pray to stay in alignment with Your great plan for my life. I ask that You give me the courage to follow the path less traveled. I pray that You open my eyes so that I do not give in to the distractions of this world. I pray my conduct reflects faithfulness to Your word and truth. In Jesus' Name, Amen."

REFLECT

What conscious behaviors do you need to stay away from?

_____

_____

_____

_____

_____

_____

_____

_____

_____

_____

_____

_____

_____

_____

_____

_____

_____

_____

_____

TODAY'S WORKOUT

WARM UP

Dynamic stretching, 5 min jog

*Following the warm up, repeat circuit in order.

Stretch well once complete.

EXERCISE	REPS
Plank w/glute kickbacks	35 sec
Alternating Front lunges	12 reps each leg
Shuffles	30 sec
Sumo Squats	15 reps
Stair step ups	60 sec
Plank knee to elbow reaches	40 sec

Perform circuit for 3 rounds.

Rest for 1-2 minutes between circuits

DAY TWELVE
ACCOUNTABILITY

"Confess your faults to one another and pray for one another so that you may be healed. The earnest prayer of a righteous person has great power and produces wonderful results."

JAMES 5:16

Without accountability there is no consequence for your inactivity! If you've gotten distracted by life and fell off track, don't worry. Today I encourage you to reach out to your support system and confess your faults. Be clear with them on how they can pray for you. Be open about how your eating habits have gotten out of control or if you're stressed and not eating. Whatever it is just be honest. Nobody in your life needs you to be perfect, they need you to be real. Then, lend a listening ear and take the time to pray for them. You must also confess your faults to God. There is healing and restoration in your confession. You are reminding yourself that you don't have it all together. This requires a humble posture. The Word tells us that God stays close to the humble. This type of humility can take you places that no weight loss pill ever can. In Romans 12:3, we are reminded not to think too highly of ourselves! To others you could appear to be the strongest one in your group of friends journeying towards total health. So, telling them you haven't worked out in a week can feel embarrassing. As you remain humble and near to God you will grow to understand the extraordinary abilities you possess in God through Christ. Confessing your faults is key to unlocking those abilities. You are not to become so puffed up with pride that you forget who and what you really need: God and His grace.

Pray with me: "God, I confess I don't make my workouts a priority. Having to exercise is daunting. I confess that I am still over-eating or skipping meals because I am anxious or not making time. I still eat until I feel comfort. Please reveal to me my brokenness in this unhealthy habit. I need Your guidance and wisdom to overcome this, God. I will be patient as You send me the right people and resources I need to be successful. I am keeping my hope in You and not in temporary fixes. I ask this in Your Son's, Jesus Christ, name, Amen."

REFLECT

Do you struggle with accountability? If so, why?

_____

_____

_____

_____

_____

_____

_____

_____

_____

_____

_____

_____

_____

_____

_____

_____

_____

_____

_____

TODAY'S WORKOUT

Rest your body!
Foam roll. Go for a walk if you wish.
Stretch for at least 20 minutes!

DAY THIRTEEN
SPIRITUAL ENDURANCE

> *"We rejoice in our sufferings, knowing that suffering produces endurance, endurance produces character and character produces life."*

ROMANS 5:3-4

Suffering produces endurance. Endurance is the ability to exert yourself and remain active for a long period of time. This means that if you keep going when it gets hard and stay the course, you **will** build enough endurance to make this a lifestyle. Because let's be honest, diets don't work. It is a temporary fix. They never get to the root of the problem. All you are doing is eliminating certain foods for a specific amount of time. When you begin a diet, you are motivated and pumped, but when the motivation goes away is when you need endurance! *Motivation can light the flame, but it can't keep it lit.* Jesus endured so **YOU** could be free. Begin today with peace, and praise God in advance for your endurance. Be careful not to rush this process. God never said we would only suffer for a few days. "So, after you have suffered a little while, he will restore, support, and strengthen you, and he will place you on a firm foundation." -1 Peter 5:10. Take a deep breath! Remember that the path of life you are in is a marathon not a sprint. You can't expect things to happen overnight. It took years for your body to become what it is now; so be humble enough to know you will not wake up in a new body in 30 days. The process can become less painful because you know what it is going to produce. Let's count it all joy.

Pray with me: "God, thank You so much for another day to build endurance. Thank You for deafening my ears to all negativity the enemy tries to use that slow me down! Thank You for divine intervention over the habits that are dying so hard. Thank You for reminding me that I am YOUR handiwork, created by You to do good works. Thank You for giving me the grace to have discipline over what I put into my body and how I move my body—to give honor to Your Holy name. In Jesus' name I pray, Amen."

REFLECT

Assess your spiritual and physical endurance today. What small thing can you do today to advance you in these areas?

_____

_____

_____

_____

_____

_____

_____

_____

_____

_____

_____

_____

_____

_____

_____

_____

_____

_____

_____

TODAY'S WORKOUT

WARM UP

Dynamic stretching, 35 sec ice skaters X2

*Following the warm up, repeat circuit in order.

EXERCISE	REPS/TIME	REST
1ST CIRCUIT		
Jackknives	15 reps	
Cross mountain climbers	20 reps	Rest 1 minute
Oblique reaches	20 reps	
Star jumps	15 reps	
2ND CIRCUIT		
Leg raises	30 reps	
X Crunches	20 reps	Rest 1 minute
Plank	45 sec	
Squat jumps	20 reps	

Perform circuit for 3 rounds. Rest for 1-2 minutes
between circuits. Stretch well once complete.

DAY FOURTEEN
COMFORT COMES FROM GOD

> *"Praise be to the God and Father of our Lord Jesus Christ, the father of compassion and the God of all comfort. Who comforts us in all of our troubles, so that we can comfort those in any trouble with the comfort we ourselves receive from God."*

2 CORINTHIANS 1: 3–4

God brings you comfort so you can comfort His people. That is why I became a trainer; because comfort can come in many forms! God gave me the tools and resources to learn how to eat right and exercise to heal my mind and body! I believe I was called to serve others in the same way. There are breakthroughs tied to my obedience. Yours too! Many times, I wanted to run to things and people. Sometimes I did, but as my mind got quieter, God's voice became clearer. At first it felt lonely, but God's presence comforted me. I felt whole — as if I needed nothing. I stopped looking to hot popcorn and wine or any person for comfort. Back then I needed comfort to know that something was happening even though I couldn't see it;

comfort to know the workouts were actually worth it. These days are when you must stay on guard against the enemy's lies. Desiring comfort can take you to a familiar place in your mind. That familiar place always leads to a familiar choice. That choice becomes a habit. To reach your goals, you have to break free from the familiar cycle.

You are strong enough to be the example. You could be breaking a generational curse of obesity in your family! Your obedience is important because the growth won't happen in your comfort zone. However, growth is definitely uncomfortable. We second-guess ourselves; we think we are in way over our heads, and we tend to think about giving up. It's during these times that we want comfort. But Listen...You are POPPIN! Okay? Be proud of your process not just the end goal. Because you are human! Most importantly, you know he's a jealous God. Don't depend on others for comfort! People will fail you, not even purposely, but they will. Sometimes your best friend won't answer the phone when it feels like you need encouragement the most; but God will be there. He is the God of all comfort. Count on Him. Shout to Him, cry out to Him! Cast your cares right now so He can comfort you. Then, one day you will be able to comfort someone else!

Pray with me: "God, wow. This is more frustrating than I expected. I do know that lasting change is expensive, and You paid a high price for me to be saved. I thank You for ending my toxic relationship with food so that I may focus on my relationship with You! I thank You for comforting me today, so I may comfort others! I am coming to You as humbly as I know how, and I am casting my cares on You because I know You care for me! Today I walk in confidence that You've given me all the strength I need. In Jesus' name, Amen."

REFLECT

What do you believe God is saying to you today?

_____

_____

_____

_____

_____

_____

_____

_____

_____

_____

_____

_____

_____

_____

_____

_____

_____

_____

TODAY'S WORKOUT

Rest your body!
Foam roll. Go for a walk if you wish.
Stretch for at least 20 minutes!

DAY FIFTEEN
STAYING COMMITTED

"But as for you, be strong and courageous, for your work will be rewarded."

DEUTERONOMY 31:6

It takes extraordinary effort to keep going after a goal when there are so many forces fighting against you. This is where you need to have a relentless belief in yourself. Believe in your abilities. Believe that God has graced you to complete everything He **needs** you to do. Other people might have something negative to say. They might feel like you started a fitness program before. They probably don't care and just want to drag you to your old ways. Rebuke it and don't let it distract you, because this isn't a diet or anything close to it. We are getting to the root of the problem. We are peeling back layers to get to our true selves. We are choosing to be strong and depend on God's promises to grant us the desires of our hearts. Not the desires of our flesh.

Don't let your commitment be based on how you feel. **Feelings are not facts; the Word of God is.** Now shoulders back, chest out. You can do this. Be STRONG today!

Pray with me: "Lord I am on a mission to be who You have called me to be. I declare that I am mentally tough. I declare that I am resilient. Father God, thank You that I am the strongest I've ever been! I know that you have already mapped out my life and I am exactly where I am supposed to be right now. Thank You for courage even in the face of opposition. Lord You are good! And I am grateful to be Your child! Thank You in Jesus' name, Amen."

REFLECT

Write down what you believe you are doing well this week and what you can do better.

_____

_____

_____

_____

_____

_____

_____

_____

_____

_____

_____

_____

_____

_____

_____

_____

_____

_____

TODAY'S WORKOUT

WARM UP
20 sec light jog; 20 sec fast high knee; 30 sec jumping jacks.
*Following the warm up, repeat leg circuit in order
with minimal rest in between exercises.

EXERCISE	REPS
Squat w/Glute kick backs	45 sec alternating
Good mornings	12 reps
Standing side leg lifts	20 each side
Bridges	20 reps then 30 sec squeeze
Reverse Lunges	45 sec
Wall sit	60 sec

Perform circuit for 3 rounds.
Rest for 1-2 minutes between circuits.
Stretch well once complete.

GOD IS A CHAIN BREAKER

"He brought them out of the darkness, the utter darkness and broke away their chains."

PSALM 107:14

You're still carrying too much. The weight you are trying to get rid of is so much more than physical! When we gain weight, there is fat trapped in our cells. So, imagine what is trapped in your mind? Imagine what is trapped in your spirit?

Is it unforgiveness, resentment, abandonment, offense, or rejection? Listen, everyone has a story.

There are certain things and experiences in your upbringing that have shaped the way you think and move through life. Sometimes we develop chains due to unfortunate events from our past. Often, we don't recognize them as a chain holding us back until they're too heavy and we can't move. Ask yourself these questions: Is there anyone in my life I need to forgive? Do I hold chains of regret from past mistakes? Do I often feel sorry for myself? Do I constantly worry about the future? Do I hold resentment or bitterness towards anyone?

The chains described above affect your thought patterns, decisions and create unrealistic expectations in your mind.

Unforgiveness can literally make you sick spiritually and physically. Years of emotional eating can create a layer of insulation around your heart, but you need to heal to be released from the false comfort. Persistent bitterness, unforgiveness and negative emotions can cause chronic anxiety. Anxiety can lead to many chemical and physical changes in the body. It produces an excess of adrenaline and cortisol. Suppression of such issues can negatively affect your appetite, immune system, blood pressure and cause inflammation. It is such a deep physical burden! These things keep your body in fight or flight mode. Therefore, you are constantly tense and stressed. Sometimes it happens subconsciously because it has become part of your identity. You can't make good decisions from a place of bitterness, anger or resentment!

Those kinds of chains can keep you bound for years. No matter what chains are weighing you down, there is good news! Those spiritual shackles will no longer dictate how you move, how you think or how you speak. Psalm 107:14 tell us, "He brought them out of the darkness, the utter darkness and broke away their chains." Don't rush your reflection time today. Let God speak to your heart and reveal what you need to do. Know that this is a process that starts with a decision. When you forgive by an act of your will and let go of the things holding you back, your shoulders will feel light as a feather! Spend as much time on this as you need to.

Pray with me: "Lord, I've identified some chains that have tormented my thoughts and crippled me with fear. Right now, I release it all to You and declare by faith that I am free. I am no longer imprisoned by any physical or spiritual chains. I ask You to break me out of this bondage, so I can begin walking in the purpose You have for me. I will move in clarity, not chaos in the name of Jesus. Your Word says that anything I loose on earth will be loosed in Heaven. Thank You, Lord! Thank You for the strength and grace to give these burdens to You completely. In Jesus' name, Amen."

REFLECT

Do your best to answer the questions from the second paragraph of devotion today honestly.

_____

_____

_____

_____

_____

_____

_____

_____

_____

_____

_____

_____

_____

_____

_____

_____

_____

TODAY'S WORKOUT

WARM UP

Dynamic stretching, 100 jumping jacks or 100 jump rope x2

*Following the warm up, repeat circuit in order.

EXERCISE	REPS
High knees	30 sec
Forearm Plank	60 sec
Burpees	30 sec
Coffin sit ups	60 sec
Jumping jacks	30 sec
Reverse Crunches	60 sec

Perform circuit for 3-4 rounds.

Rest for 20-30 sec between exercises. Rest for 1-2 minutes between rounds. Stretch well once complete.

DAY SEVENTEEN
YOU CAN DO ALL THINGS

"For I can do all things through Christ, who gives me strength."

PHILIPPIANS 4:13

Make this verse the song in your heart. It's your hope. It's your strength. This verse reminds you that you are a soldier, and you can. God has a never-ending supply of courage and strength to give to you.

Your circumstances do not dictate your level of joy! What Paul teaches us in Philippians 4 is contentment. The dictionary definition of content is "in a state of peaceful happiness". That means no matter what, be content in your one-piece swimsuit; be content eating your salad; be content in your one-bedroom apartment; be content in every season of life! It's important to read the verses that come before this line that instantly boosts our confidence. The context of scripture is what brings us clarity. The "all things" that Paul mentions really means that no matter what it looks like, we can do it AND God is faithful to give us the strength to do it all. We have to dust off the glitter surrounding this verse and fall in love with being content. Nope, it's not easy. At all. It is a process that we learn; but be encouraged by this: Paul wrote one of the most encouraging Bible verses IN JAIL. He wasn't on a beach being fed grapes with a Mimosa in his hand. You can be in one of the darkest seasons of your life or be in a season of consecutive wins. You can do ALL things in both seasons. Receive the strength available to you! Go back and read your goals from day one and get to it.

Pray with me: "Father God, teach me to be content in the body You have given me. Teach me how to be satisfied by the truth of Your words! Help me be content in what You have given me in my home, career and family life! I don't want to focus on what I don't have or what the world tells me I should have. Protect me from comparing my body, my job, my home, my family or my material possessions to others in Jesus' name. Remind me daily that I can do all things through You! Remind me that I can fight for the home I want, the body I want and the career I want while being content with what I have now! Help me remember Your faithful provision and unfailing love. Thank You! In Jesus' name, Amen."

REFLECT

What does being content feel like to you?

_____

_____

_____

_____

_____

_____

_____

_____

_____

_____

_____

_____

_____

_____

_____

_____

TODAY'S WORKOUT

WARM UP

20 sec light jog; 20 sec fast high knee; 30 sec plank jacks.
*Following the warm up, repeat arm circuit in order
with minimal rest in between exercises.

EXERCISE	REPS
Mountain Climbers	40 sec
Tricep Dips	20 reps
Inch worm	35 sec
Wide Push ups	12 reps
Superman with reach	40 sec
Crab kicks	30 sec

Perform circuit for 3 rounds.
Rest for 1-2 minutes between circuits.
Stretch well once complete.

DAY EIGHTEEN
LEARN TO SOAR

"But those that trust in the Lord will find new strength. They will soar high on wings like eagles. They will run and not grow weary. They will walk and not faint."

ISAIAH 40:31

The Lord says we will soar high like eagles. Eagles are the most magnificent bird in the sky. We have a lot to learn from them, especially in this scripture. Did you know that eagles can soar without flapping their wings? God made eagles so special they can literally soar through the sky for long periods of time without tremendous physical effort. **But** it takes time to build that ability; **it requires waiting**! The wings they are born with are so heavy and large that they must learn how to use thermal winds in their favor to carry them to their destination. They wait for thermals, so the air currents don't deplete them. Otherwise, they could die by exhausting their energy from flapping away. Because of waiting, eagles learn to soar with perfect ease.

Amazing right? The wings of the eagles represent our faith and belief in the Lord. Have you ever been working so hard toward something that you were constantly getting burned out and losing hope?

You may need to get in alignment with God and let the Holy Spirit be your wind to propel you forward. When you are doing what you are graced to do and not overworking yourself, you will see the power in what the Lord has already placed inside of you. You will see that you already have all you need to soar. Let's learn to be led by the Holy Spirit, not your flesh. "It is not by force nor by strength, but by my Spirit, says the Lord of heaven's armies" –Zechariah 4:6. Yes, faith without works is dead, so physically you must put in the work and move *your* body. Some of us are trying to wake up in someone else's body and that just will not happen. The pounds are not going to supernaturally fall off. There is still effort required of you but you must do the work while operating in the Spirit. You will be successful when you completely trust Him to carry you. Trusting in your flesh will lead you to sin, then you won't be a good steward over the body you've been given. Let's wait for the right wind like the eagle so we can soar into our best self!

Pray with me: "God, I trust that You didn't make any mistakes when You made me. I have enough faith and belief in my Lord and Savior to keep my confidence. May the Holy Spirit guide me, empower me and give me enough strength to soar gracefully like an eagle! Teach me O God! Show me the areas in my life where I am depending on my own might and reveal it to me. I know that Your power works best in my weakness. In Jesus' name, Amen."

REFLECT

What do you believe God is saying to you today?

TODAY'S WORKOUT

WARM UP

30 sec fast high knee; 20 sec pulse squat, 30 sec jumping jacks. X2

*Following the warm up, repeat circuit in order.

EXERCISE	REPS
Russian Twists	30 reps
Cross flutter Kicks	30 reps
Alternating side lunges	35 sec
Bodyweight Plank rows	40 sec
Froggers	12 reps
Tabletop bridges	15 reps

Perform circuit for 3 rounds.

Rest for 1-2 minutes between circuits.

Stretch well once complete.

FOOD IS A GIFT

"I have told you all this so that you may have peace in me. Here on earth you will have many trials and sorrows. But take heart, because I have overcome the world."

JOHN 16:33

Nothing you are struggling with is a surprise to God. He has a victory for everything you think is unchangeable. You cannot let anything going on in the world take the peace that God has given you. The power that is in us is greater than any power coming against us!

We know that every good thing comes from God. Food is definitely one of those gifts. In today's society, we have become so obsessed with it and anxious about it that it creates a daily struggle in our lives. The enemy wants to use every tool possible to distract us from being satisfied by God. While it's important to throw out the foods in your kitchen that harm your body, it's important for you to realize that this is a spiritual battle. Satan wants you to keep ignoring your hunger for Christ by making you full on empty calories and temporary satisfaction. Food is not your enemy. The enemy is your enemy. Let's awaken your hunger for God so that when trials come, you handle them appropriately-- with God, not food.

Today, choose to trust and stand on His promises and give thanks so He can guide you to victory. If you are constantly worrying about things, it negatively affects your mental health, which creates a domino effect. When you are feeling worried or stressed, you are less focused and less likely to work out and choose the right foods. Keep the chaos of the world out of your sight. All things are possible in God, through God and by God! Fix your thoughts on what is true. Read Philippians 4:8.

Pray with me: "Father God, thank You! Thank You for peace! I trust that as I put my hope in You and not a diet or quick fix, that You'll continue to teach me how to release the physical and mental pounds, in Jesus' name. Lord, You are good! Order my steps today and every day to come. Keep me in Your perfect peace.

In Jesus' name, Amen."

REFLECT

Would you describe your relationship with food negative or positive?

_____

_____

_____

_____

_____

_____

_____

_____

_____

_____

_____

_____

_____

_____

_____

_____

_____

_____

_____

_____

_____

_____

TODAY'S WORKOUT

Rest your body!
Foam roll. Go for a walk if you wish.
Stretch for at least 20 minutes!

NO MORE SHAME

"Fear not, you will no longer live in shame. Don't be afraid; there is no more disgrace for you. You will no longer remember the shame of your youth."

ISAIAH 54:4

God is your redeemer! No more shame. Shame is a painful emotion. It is usually caused by some past mistake, shortcoming or guilt. It's easy to begin to feel shame along your fitness journey. You may feel ashamed for gaining the weight in the first place. You may feel ashamed that you've lost the weight before and gained it back. You may feel ashamed that you haven't been able to fully commit to it in the past. But God wants to take the shame off you because it is keeping you stuck. The enemy knows that if he can condemn you he can slow you down. **No matter who or what makes you feel condemned your value has not changed to God.** Today we need to slow down and reflect on what *shame* we could be carrying. It is important to identify it, so we can release it to God. You've been relinquishing control. You have been releasing burdens and forgiving people. I'm so proud of you and you should be proud of yourself! It's a great start, but there can still be more!

Now, you must let go of all the baggage you are carrying because it could be preventing you from demonstrating the fruits of the spirit. Write it all down today. Take your time. You cannot walk in self-control if you are not confident in who you are.

"I am ashamed of..." I feel shame when..."

Once we identify the shame we can ask God to lift it all off us. Then we can move forward towards wholeness. God is the only one who can make us whole, not our spouse, children, accomplishments, or anything else. Let's be intentional about not looking to external sources to fill a void.

Pray with me: "Lord, thank You for giving me fresh revelation. Thank You for giving me a fresh love for myself! I thank You for being my Holy Redeemer, so that I no longer need to live in shame. I ask that You help me to identify any shame that I am carrying so it can be released. I am praising You in advance for the victory to come from this exercise. I will no longer believe the shameful things others have placed on me and the shame I've placed on myself. I thank You for allowing me to draw near to You so that I may experience total cleansing and forgiveness by Your Spirit. In Jesus' name, Amen."

REFLECT

Identify all shame you may be living with below.

_____

_____

_____

_____

_____

_____

_____

_____

_____

_____

_____

_____

_____

_____

_____

_____

_____

_____

_____

TODAY'S WORKOUT

WARM UP

Dynamic stretching, 35 sec ice skaters X2

*Following the warm up, repeat circuit in order.

EXERCISE	REPS/TIME	REST
1ST CIRCUIT		
Jackknives	15 reps	
Cross mountain climbers	15 reps	Rest 1 minute
Oblique reaches	15 reps	
Star jumps	15 reps	
2ND CIRCUIT		
Leg raises	15 reps	
X Crunches	15 reps	Rest 1 minute
Plank	60 sec	
Squat jumps	15 reps	

Perform circuit for 5 rounds.

Stretch well once complete.

DAY TWENTY-ONE
SELF-DISCIPLINE BREEDS SUCCESS

"For God has not given us the spirit of fear and timidity but of power, love, and self-discipline."

2 TIMOTHY 1:7

To achieve anything in life it will require a certain level of discipline. Discipline is defined as the ability to control one's feelings and overcome one's weaknesses. Can you easily identify your weaknesses? There was a dark season in my life when my feelings used to control my entire day. I was convinced I was incapable of controlling my anger. My words and actions matched those thoughts. Do you know what that's like? Well, there is hope! The more I got to know God for myself I realized how powerful I was. I realized I had authority, and could tap into it whenever I needed to. Unlike others who eat when they are feeling emotional, I wouldn't eat at all. I lacked the discipline to eat even when my body needed nutrients. I realized that something had to change. Then I committed to moving forward no matter what. I chose to believe that the same power that rose Jesus from the dead was living within me. I knew I needed to be disciplined enough to nourish my body and move my body even when I didn't feel like it.

God has given you the power to demonstrate the fruit of self-discipline as well. Paul teaches us that we are not running the race of life for a physical trophy but for the reward that is in heaven. So you have to be disciplined enough to move your body! When you exercise you are releasing endorphins, reducing stress, improving blood flow, strengthening your muscles, allowing more oxygen to flow to your brain and so much more!! **We must spend time disciplining our spirit so that we may discipline our mind and body.**

When you're running long distance it's not how you start, it's how you finish! Disciplining your spirit comes from habits that you make to draw near to God through prayer, reading scripture, fasting, and worship.

Pray with me: "Father God, I am longing to operate in the fruits of the spirit. I ask that You help me put my spirit in charge so that I will continue to submit to my spirit and not my flesh. Today and every day to come I present my body as a living sacrifice to You, Lord. I know that my flesh will lead me to sin. Today I put my spirit in the driver's seat and I commit to be a doer of Your Word. I will control my flesh and operate by my spirit. Today I pray for the fruit of self-control to govern my impulses especially with food. Thank You for the grace and strength to do so. In Jesus' name, Amen."

REFLECT

When you think of discipline do you consider yourself successful based on what you are NOT doing? Real discipline is focusing on what you ARE doing. Consider this difference below.

_____

_____

_____

_____

_____

_____

_____

_____

_____

_____

_____

_____

_____

_____

_____

TODAY'S WORKOUT

Rest your body!
Foam roll. Go for a walk if you wish.
Stretch for at least 20 minutes!

DAY TWENTY-TWO
DON'T RUSH

"So, let's not get tired of doing what is good. At just the right time we will reap a harvest of blessing if we don't give up."

GALATIANS 6:9

To reap a harvest, you must sow, but there is a time of waiting in between the two. Eating clean and consistently exercising is your seed-time. Keep going relentlessly and don't give up. You will reap what you've sown. Don't rush this or try to harvest your crop before it's ready. Do you know what's more important than not giving up? Keeping your eyes on Jesus! God has so much for you, but He needs you to keep your eyes fixed on His truth and not your circumstances. If we take our eyes off Jesus, we risk letting the world bring us down. He is an all-knowing God. He knows exactly what you are experiencing. He knows that you are uncomfortable. He is more concerned with your focus than your situation. The blessing you are waiting to receive is directly tied to your obedience and focus. The *best* part? God only requires progress not perfection. **You don't need to have it all figured out right now. You just need to keep your eyes on the One who does!** Hebrews 6:12 reminds us that it's through faith and patience that we inherit the promises of God!!

Pray with me: "Lord, help me not get distracted by the woes of my day-to-day stress. Help me not to base my joy on my circumstance. Lord, please implant in me a laser focus that is honorable to You. I have given up on my goals before and I refuse to do it again. With Your help I know that I can keep going. Allow me to respect the seeds that I am planting and not rush their process to sprout. Teach me how to maintain and sustain my focus. In Jesus' name, Amen."

REFLECT

What do you believe God is saying to you today?

_____

_____

_____

_____

_____

_____

_____

_____

_____

_____

_____

_____

_____

_____

_____

_____

_____

_____

_____

_____

TODAY'S WORKOUT

WARM UP

Dynamic stretching, light 5-minute jog
*Following the warm up, repeat leg circuit in order
for 2-3 rounds. Stretch well once complete.

EXERCISE	REPS/TIME	REST
Squat w/knee up crunch	35 sec	
Star jumps	20 sec	
Donkey kicks	25 each leg	
Fire hydrant	20 each leg	Aim to only
Straight leg pulse	20 each leg	rest in between
Squat jumps	30 sec	entire circuit
Lunges	15 each leg	
Deadlifts	15 reps	
Squat pulse	20 reps	

DAY TWENTY-THREE
YOU ARE FREE INDEED

"So if the son sets you free, you will be free indeed."

JOHN 8:36

Most of us have grown up addicted to the taste of sugar and salt. Like it or not, we aren't supposed to always eat for taste, we are supposed to eat to live! Shift your mind and know that God can deliver you from any addiction no matter how small you think it is. If it is distracting you from your purpose, it needs to go!

You may be reading this like, 'I don't have an addiction, this doesn't apply to me.' The cup of coffee with 2 creams and 4 sugars that you stop and get on your way to work EVERY morning is an addiction. That Pepsi you buy when you are up late studying or finishing reports, that's an addiction. That bag of chips you buy EVERY time you put gas in your car is an addiction. That snack you make when you're at home and not even hungry is an addiction. You get it, right? Old habits do die hard, but that does not make them impossible to overcome. I want you to be healthy. I want you to be free—free from worry, free from doubt, free from diseases, and free from addiction too.

Take a step back and think about all the extras in your life. The unnecessary rituals or foods, drinks, or habits that aren't aiding in your healthy lifestyle change and write them in your reflect section for today. Then write what you are going to replace them with. If it's a cup of coffee with extra sugar, replace it with a green tea and lemon. If it's a handful of jelly beans before bed, grab frozen grapes or take the extra few minutes instead of adding inches to your waist line and study the Word. Be still, be quiet and listen. Write the small changes you want to make. Write the vision, make it plain! Read Habakkuk 2:2. Consider operating in the 90/10 rule! 90% of the time you should devote to healthy living and maintenance and 10% of the time you could enjoy trying new restaurants, birthday parties, celebrations, etc. This is where we are mindful of portion sizes and leave room for life to happen and fun! There are many people reading this who live by 10/90 and that is how it gets dangerous. The 10/90 lifestyle breeds hypertension, diabetes, depression, and everything we do not want. Think about what percentage you are living in. Don't be afraid to start with 80/20. The goal should be to live a healthy balanced life!

Pray with me: "Lord, thank You for humbling me long enough for me to identify my poor habits and rituals. Thank You for giving me authority over them so that I am not controlled by them. Thank You for teaching me to slow down and be still so I can recognize this cycle. I put all the unsanctified and unholy parts of me under the rule of Jesus right now. I renounce the ways I have presented my appetite and drinking to sin. I present my eating and drinking habits to Jesus right now. I break the enemy's stronghold on me and I know that the blood of Jesus cleanses me of everything!! Holy Spirit guide me and keep me protected from the enemy that is lurking around looking for someone to devour. Thank You, Lord! In Jesus' name, Amen."

REFLECT

Write down all the unhealthy extras in your life. What can you eliminate or replace them with?

_____

_____

_____

_____

_____

_____

_____

_____

_____

_____

_____

_____

_____

_____

_____

_____

_____

_____

_____

TODAY'S WORKOUT

WARM UP

30 sec ice skaters; 30 sec fast high knee; 30 sec burpees. X2
*Following the warm up, repeat leg circuit in order
with minimal rest in between exercises.

EXERCISE	REPS
Mountain Climbers	150 reps (left and right is one)
Leg raises	100 reps
High knees	150 reps
Coffin sit ups	100 reps
Squat Jacks	100 reps
Plank crunches	100 reps

You can choose to split up the reps by 4 rounds.
Stretch well once complete.

DAY TWENTY-FOUR
GOD'S GRACE IS SUFFICIENT

"My grace is all you need. My power works best in weakness.
So now I am glad to boast about my weaknesses, so that the
power of Christ can work through me."

2 CORINTHIANS 12:9

We're taught to be strong and constantly keep a smile. While that is very good we need to learn how to be vulnerable with God. We need to learn how to say, "God I am not strong right now, I don't have all the answers and I don't know what to do next." He wants us to lean on Him. We can get so caught up in being the strong woman or strong man that we block our blessings. Sometimes we may feel like, 'I did this to myself I must stay strong and face it'. The thing about grace is we don't earn it! Repent of your sins so God can cast them out into the sea of forgetfulness! God is not upset with you.

By recognizing you are weak, God will give you the strength you need. By recognizing you need help and saying you do not have the power to move that mountain on your own, God will give you the tools you need to complete the task and move in the spirit. By going to God and placing all your issues at His feet you will be empowered and clothed in strength! You have been going strong on this journey for more than 3 weeks! Things are slowly beginning to align in your life. Don't fret. Frustration is normal. This process is good! All good things come from God. The enemy wants to steal, kill and destroy every good thing in your life, but God wants you to resist the devil. Continue to care for your temple and remember that your weakness gives you power. Your weakness keeps you humble. Your weakness brings you closer to God!

Pray with me: "Thank You, Lord! I praise You that this weakness is not forever, and it doesn't define me! Lord, thank You for being my rock. You know the burdens I carry. Lord help me to embrace my weaknesses, so I can trust You with them! Send me joy during this struggle, Lord! Thank You! in Jesus Christ's name, Amen."

REFLECT

Write a letter to God recording your most vulnerable moments from this week.

_____

_____

_____

_____

_____

_____

_____

_____

_____

_____

_____

_____

_____

_____

_____

_____

_____

_____

_____

TODAY'S WORKOUT

WARM UP
20 sec fast high knee; 30 sec plank jacks. X2
*Following the warm up, repeat arm circuit in order
with minimal rest in between exercises.

EXERCISE	REPS
Mountain Climbers/tall plank	30 sec/30 sec
Tricep Dips	20 reps
Inch worm	45 sec
Wide Push ups	15 reps
Superman with back squeeze	45 sec
Crab kicks	35 sec

Perform circuit for 3 rounds.
Rest for 1-2 minutes between circuits.
Stretch well once complete.

YOU ARE GOD'S HANDIWORK

"For we are God's handiwork, created in Christ Jesus to do good works, which he prepared for us in advance to do."

EPHESIANS 2:10

D on't you understand how special you are? You become His masterpiece by His grace.

When we commit to the good works He prepared for us we become an example of His power, goodness, love, peace and joy! We just need to receive the grace and strength to walk it out! Notice I said receive. That is a choice! Everyone has the opportunity to walk in the prosperous life that God set before them, but everyone doesn't choose to *receive* His grace. While you walk in His grace, know that God hears you where your heart is. Your energy and effort matters. When you draw near to God, He draws near to you! Now, check your heart, are you communicating with God on a higher level?

Consider this: God needs you to be strong for His Kingdom. He has something specific He needs you to carry out and bring to fruition. If you are always tired and lethargic how will you complete any mission He's given you? How will you walk in the obedience that it requires to fulfill your purpose if you always give in to your flesh?

Your body is only going to be as strong as the foods you put into it. Stay qualified and disciplined. You are God's handiwork! What a special honor! If you aren't healthy you will miss out on opportunities to change your life and the lives of those around you.

Pray with me: "Thank You, Lord! Sometimes I forget how important I am to You. Sometimes I try to win Your love by working hard. I want to fulfill the plan You have for me and be an agent of change in the Body of Christ, but I fall short and forget to take care of myself first as You told me to do. Lord, Your power and grace are so mighty and sufficient for every situation in my life! Help me to boldly and confidently draw near to You. Help me to look at my mess as an opportunity to grow in You. Lord, I want to rest in Your power and receive Your grace. Thank You. In Jesus' name, Amen."

REFLECT

What do you believe God is saying to you today?

_____

_____

_____

_____

_____

_____

_____

_____

_____

_____

_____

_____

_____

_____

_____

_____

_____

_____

TODAY'S WORKOUT

WARM UP
Dynamic stretching, 5 min jog
*Following the warm up, repeat circuit in order.
Stretch well once complete.

EXERCISE	REPS
Plank w/glute kickbacks	45 sec
Alternating Front lunges	30 sec each leg
Shuffles	30 sec
Sumo Squats w/calf raise	20 reps
Stair step ups	60 sec
Plank knee to elbow reaches	45 sec

Perform circuit for 3 rounds.
Rest for 1-2 minutes between circuits

DAY TWENTY-SIX
NO MORE EXCUSES

"When Jesus saw him and knew he had been ill for a long
time, he asked him, "Would you like to get well?"

JOHN 5:6

D o you really want to be free? Do you really want to release the
weight? If we are not careful we can just wish for something
instead of going out and taking it. We can be so blinded by
our circumstances that we make excuses as to why we can't achieve
something, and our identity becomes lost in the pain. In chapter 5
of the Book of John, Jesus found a sick man by a pool. The pool was
a supernatural place where people would go to get healed. An angel
would stir the waters and the first to jump in was always healed.
Jesus walked up to the pool by a man that had been sick for 38 years.
Jesus asked the man, "Do you want to get well?" Instead of the man
screaming out, "Yes! Of course, please help me and push me into the
pool!!' The man replied, "I can't sir…for I have no one to put me into
the pool when the water bubbles up. Someone else always gets there
ahead of me." This is a victim mentality. Woe is me. I can't do this.
I can't do that. I need someone to help me. The man had been sick
for so long that he couldn't even see the possibility of being healed.

So many people are trapped by this defeated mindset. When you feel powerless you lose hope in God and start putting your hope in quick fixes. For this reason, Americans spend more than 50 BILLION dollars per year on weight loss programs, diets and supplements. Do you want to lose weight? "Yes, but I have knee problems and my back went out last year; every time I eat spinach I gag; I can't afford a gym or trainer, and I don't do breakfast at all." Sound like anyone you know? Those responses are excuses. The question was do you want to lose weight? Are you operating in a victim mentality in your finances? In your relationships? As a parent? God's grace is enough for you! Even though we can look at this text and feel this man had so many excuses, Jesus saw fit to heal him anyway. God wants to surround you with grace regardless of how unworthy you feel! You no longer have to look to the left or the right. It does not matter who is ahead of you when God's grace is on your life! Take your time and examine the excuses that are shrinking your faith. Choose victory!

Pray with me: "Father God, thank You for sending Your son to die for me so I can have victory! Thank You for showing me the ways in which I carry a victim mentality. Thank You for giving me authority to break down the barriers in my mind. Thank You for removing the mess from my mind so I may stand firm in Your truth and Your glory! Thank You for delivering me from this constant wrestling with the enemy!

Thank You for reminding me that I am a child of the Most High King and I deserve to live a life of joy and abundance! Thank You for giving me the power to manifest miracles in my body, my home and my finances in Jesus' name. Thank You for giving me hope. Thank You for healing me from trauma so that I will no longer produce a victim mentality. Thank You for bondage being broken even now. Thank You for freedom and prosperity. In Jesus' name, Amen."

REFLECT

Write down your excuses to not workout or eat well, even the "legitimate" ones.

TODAY'S WORKOUT

WARM UP
Dynamic stretching, 150 jumping jacks or 150 jump rope x2
*Following the warm up, repeat circuit in order.

EXERCISE	REPS
High knees	30 sec
Plank twists	60 sec
Burpees	30 sec
Coffin sit ups	60 sec
Jumping jacks	30 sec
Reverse Crunches	60 sec

Perform circuit for 3-4 rounds.
Rest for 20-30 sec between exercises. Rest for 1-2 minutes between rounds. Stretch well once complete.

DAY TWENTY-SEVEN
EAT FOR HIS GLORY

"So whatever you eat or drink, or whatever you do, do it all for the glory of God."

1 CORINTHIANS 10:31

Besides sin, everything we do has the ability to be done for the glory of God. Eating and exercising should never be deemed so secular that you feel like you can't do it for God. In all things, you are to live for God. This rule is sufficient for all of us to remain mindful of what we consume. So much of what we eat and drink serves no great purpose, nor does it bring honor to God. We eat too many things that are genetically modified. Everything from the Lord contains a seed! Watermelons, cucumbers, radishes, lemons, apples, oranges, I could go on. Even humans have seeds! We have been given all these wonderful things, so they can multiply. There is nothing lacking in the Body of Christ. Let's keep it simple with this game changing quote from Michael Pollan, "Eat real food, mostly plants, not too much." We are always sure to wash our vegetables before we eat them because we are so careful of what we consume into our stomach. But are we as careful of what is consumed into our hearts? Seriously, what does my heart have to do with me losing weight? I do squats, I eat spinach and drink water! In Mark chapter 7, Jesus teaches about inner purity. Basically, you can eat all the Brussels sprouts and do all the jumping jacks you want but if you don't address what is going on in your heart you will never be whole. You need to be well in order to walk fully in the calling God has placed on your life! Jesus says "It's not what goes into your body that defiles you; you are defiled by what comes from your heart." Let us not be confused by this and believe we can eat Oreo's for breakfast. We know that will not bring success or a slim waist. "And then he added, It is what comes from within, out of a person's heart, come evil thoughts, sexual immorality, theft, murder, adultery, greed, wickedness, deceit, lustful desires, envy, slander, pride and foolishness. All these vile things come from within; they are what defile you." Mark 7:20-22. One step at a time. One day at a time. Be mindful enough today not to consume foods that won't go bad for a whole year. I believe we should honor God with what we eat and drink! You need to be whole to make the right decisions.

Pray with me: "Lord, thank You for giving me strength to say no to my destructive habits and cravings that do my body no good! I want to acknowledge You in all my ways and honor You by what I choose to put into the body You've given me. Teach me Your wisdom regarding my health. Help me grow in my ability to cook foods that will help me operate in a spirit of excellence. Help me love the foods that love me back. Continue to guide me as I let Your word be the blueprint for this journey of health and wellness. Give me the desire to choose foods that bring vitality, natural energy, and clarity to my mind and body. Thank You in Jesus' name, Amen."

REFLECT

If you could put your nutrition habits on this scale of 90/10 being the best and 10/90 being the worst, where would you fall this week?

TODAY'S WORKOUT

Rest your body!
Foam roll. Go for a walk if you wish.
Stretch for at least 20 minutes!

DAY TWENTY-EIGHT
WALK IN WISDOM

"The wise are mightier than the strong, and those with knowledge grow stronger and stronger."

PROVERBS 24:5

The world is full of distractions and noise, but it is our inner voice of wisdom that eliminates the confusion. Wisdom is listening to God and carrying out what He tells us to do. Jesus being the foundation of our faith helps us navigate through life. Solomon went to God for wisdom and discernment and laid out his concerns. That level of humility pleased God and He encourages us to ask for wisdom because He will answer our prayers. Hosea 4:6 tell us, "for lack of knowledge my people will fail." (KJV) With wisdom you grow stronger by each experience. A fool is someone who knows the right path to take and still goes the opposite way. Have you ever found yourself in a season where it's like, "I know exactly what I need to do, but I'm just not doing it"? Let me be transparent and say I've been there. It kept me stuck for longer than I want to admit, and we all know that doesn't produce good fruit. Today you need to trust your inner voice. Trust that you can find answers and wisdom in the Word of God. Trust that if you need direction the Lord will guide you to make the wisest decision. Deep down, you know what to do. You know what's not right for your body or mental health. And whenever you aren't sure, know that you are a child of God and your foundation is Jesus. Meditate on Jeremiah 7:23–24.

Pray with me: "Father God, I ask that You give me a heart of wisdom and allow me to flee from my wicked ways. Give me a heart that is willing to obey Your Word and teachings. Keep me from ungoldly counsel and direction. Lord, keep me from following the easiest path with least resistance. Build my faith muscles to allow me to follow You! Lord, I declare by faith that my prayers will be accomplished. In Jesus' name, Amen."

REFLECT

What does wisdom mean to you? How can you apply it today?

_____

_____

_____

_____

_____

_____

_____

_____

_____

_____

_____

_____

_____

_____

_____

_____

_____

_____

TODAY'S WORKOUT

WARM UP

20 sec light jog; 20 sec fast high knee; 30 sec jumping jacks. X2
*Following the warm up, repeat leg circuit in order
with minimal rest in between exercises.

EXERCISE	REPS
Squat w/Glute kick backs	60 sec
Good mornings	60 sec
Standing side leg lifts	30 sec each side
Bridges	25 reps with 30 sec squeeze
Inner thigh leg lifts	20 each side
Wall sit	60 sec

Perform circuit for 3 rounds.
Rest for 1-2 minutes between circuits.
Stretch well once complete.

DAY TWENTY-NINE
YOU'RE WORKING FOR GOD

"Working willingly at whatever you do, as though you were
working for the Lord rather than for people."

COLOSSIANS 3:23

True health and wellness is something we want to keep for the rest of our lives! Think longevity. You can't just do the bare minimum when you want to lose 50lbs and KEEP it off or get off your blood pressure medication. You certainly can't do something just to please other people. We all know how being a people pleaser ends- not well. Do this for you. Do this because you know that the work you are putting in is glorifying God! Do this because you are taking steps to further the Kingdom! Begin today with a tall confident posture that you don't need to please anyone but the Lord. Let His grace and mercy overflow from your heart! Love God and love yourself then everything else will work itself out! Don't prioritize your to do list but make a list of your priorities first. You are a King's Kid, remember whom you report to!

Pray with me: "Lord, help me not to center my goals around vanity, my children, my spouse, my family or friends. Remind me that I am getting healthy to serve You and to glorify Your name with my obedience! If I continue striving to please people I know that it will prevent me from doing what You have called me to do, God. Thank You for this life You have given me, Lord. I know that You created me to live an abundant life for Your glory. Interrupt me when I begin living for anyone else.

Thank You for being my shield, in Jesus' name, Amen."

REFLECT

What do you believe God is saying to you today?

TODAY'S WORKOUT

WARM UP

30 sec standing oblique crunches; 30 sec fast
high knee; 35 sec plank jacks. X2
*Following the warm up, repeat arm circuit in order.
Stretch well once complete.

EXERCISE	REPS
Shoulder taps	45 sec
Tricep dips	20 reps
Tricep push ups	35 sec
Plank walk ups	45 sec
Superman with reach	45 sec
Side planks	35 sec each side

Perform circuit for 3 rounds.
Rest for 1-2 minutes between each.

DAY THIRTY
GOD HAS A PURPOSE FOR YOU

"For I know the plans I have for you, declares the Lord, plans
for welfare and not for evil, to give you a future and a hope."

JEREMIAH 29:11

YOU MATTER! God loves you. He created you on purpose and for a purpose. You are no mistake, no accident. God knows how many hairs are on your head. Know that by following God, He doesn't wish to bring you harm. When you face a difficult season, you can be confident that no weapon formed against you shall prosper. You do not have to fall back into your old ways when you experience turbulence in life. You already know where that path leads! Decide in advance what you are going to do. "I am going to enjoy my healthy meal even if I am offered pizza in the break room." "No matter what happens today God is still God." These may seem like fluffy affirmations but leading your thoughts helps to rewire them. Therefore, you need to wake up and command your day. Fill yourself with His love and truth before you do anything. Don't just let life happen to you. Be proactive instead of reactive. The enemy will attempt to make you feel worthless or as if things will never change. But you can command your mind to think positively and not be overtaken by lies in your head! God convicts with love; the enemy brings you condemnation and fear.

In every season of your life God is with you and He is the same. He still wants you to take care of yourself even if you have to spend 12 hours a day next to a loved one in the hospital bed. Even though the detours of life are confusing He STILL has a plan and it STILL is to prosper you.

Lastly, remember that we serve a God of order! Every single time you step into a new season you need to recreate order. Order can be defined as an arrangement, a system, or organization. Your entire life flows from one process to the next. Make room for your blessing by getting your life in order! Anyone can lose weight, but it takes a solid system to release it for good. Everything you did to get healed, you must continue doing to stay healed! This is a lifestyle: Prayers up, Weight Down!

Pray with me: "Thank You, Lord, for redeeming me from the hand of the enemy. Lead me to honor You in everything so that I can live a healthy life that glorifies You. Help me be the master of my thoughts and words. I thank You for the amazing plan and purpose that You have for me! I thank You that this is just the beginning of my journey of wholeness! Let me remember the blessings You have already given me, like the joy in being content. Thank You for clarity, Father. Thank You for peace. Open the horizons of my mind and heart so I may continue digging deeper and not give up. Thank You, Lord. In Jesus Christ's name, Amen."

REFLECT

Detail what you've learned about yourself in the past 30 days.

_____

_____

_____

_____

_____

_____

_____

_____

_____

_____

_____

_____

_____

_____

_____

_____

_____

_____

_____

_____

_____

TODAY'S WORKOUT

WARM UP

Dynamic stretching and 150 jumping jacks or 150 jump rope. X2

EXERCISE	REPS
Russian Twists	60 sec
Cross flutter Kicks	60 sec
Alternating side lunges	60 sec
Bodyweight Plank rows	60 sec
Froggers	30 sec
Tabletop bridges	60 sec

Perform circuit for 3 rounds.

Rest for 1-2 minutes between circuits.

Stretch well once complete.

TOOLS FOR SUCCESS

WHAT DOES IT MEAN TO EAT CLEAN?

Eating clean is simply the practice of avoiding processed and refined foods and basing your diet on whole foods. To fully maximize your results and reach your goals you must learn the discipline and consistency! You will slip up, we are humans and born to make mistakes but it's how you rise after falling. Just never give up! Eat for your specific goals! If you want to lose weight, you need to eat like it!

5 RULES TO TRANSFORM YOUR BODY:

6. Never miss a Monday: this is your opportunity to RE-FOCUS!
7. Eat 4-5x a day: this will surely increase your metabolism.
8. Be proud of your progress. Slow progress is still progress.
9. Trust the process, it will be worth it.
10. Never give up. If it were easy, everyone would do it.

WHAT DO I AVOID?

Processed foods: they are full of extra sodium, sugar and saturated fat. Avoid refined sugars, salt, soda, chips, candy, high fructose corn syrup, and mayonnaise. Reduce alcohol intake: it dehydrates you and adds extra calories to your diet. Also take note of sugars added to healthier foods like yogurt, choose plain varieties and use natural sweeteners: strawberries, blueberries, apple or banana slices. Choose tomato sauces with no added sugar. Avoid the center aisles when grocery shopping. Eliminate canned foods and go towards the fresh produce section. Pay attention to labels, just because it has fewer calories does not mean it's good for you. Choose products with the least amount of ingredients. MEAL PREP like you get paid for it. The reward of health is worth a couple hours of your time each week. It will also save you money and who doesn't want to save money? Try not to reward yourself with food, you are not a dog. Eat to live, don't live to eat. Smile more, make sleep a priority, and drink more water. Exercise is one of the most underused anti-depressants!

NUTRITION FACTS:

MACRONUTRIENTS? These consist of carbohydrates, fats, and protein! Each macronutrient is essential to life, and provides a certain amount of calories. Fat is the most calorie dense nutrient, providing 9 calories per gram. Carbohydrates and protein both provide 4 calories per gram.

TRUTH ABOUT CARBS: Carbs are your body's main source of energy! Every single source of carbohydrate falls somewhere on the Glycemic Index, which is a scale of how fast the carbs from that food enter the bloodstream. High GI foods, like sugary drinks and white bread, enter the bloodstream quickly, whereas lower GI foods, such as most fruits and whole grains, enter the blood at a slower and steadier pace. They also improve your brain function. Carbs that do your body good: bananas, apples, strawberries, oats, sweet potatoes, quinoa, Ezekiel bread, all veggies, lentils, beans, brown rice and more!

TRUTH ABOUT PROTEIN: Protein provides energy for the body. It helps your body build and repairs cells and body tissue. Protein is made up of tiny building blocks of amino acids. There are 20 amino acids and 9 are considered essential and must be obtained through food. Animal protein does fuel the muscle growth process! However, there are some foods other than animal proteins that are considered "complete proteins" because they contain all 9 amino acids. For example: quinoa, Ezekiel bread, chia seeds, hummus, beans, lentils, etc. But protein can be found in oatmeal, spinach, black beans and more! As an active adult research shows that your body needs more protein daily to repair exercise induced muscle damage. Whether you are vegetarian/vegan/pescatarian or carnivore you need protein! Studies suggest 0.7-1 gram of protein per pound of **your** body weight.

TRUTH ABOUT FATS: Fatty acids are an essential nutrient in the body! Omega 3 fatty acids carry many benefits for your body. Ex: reducing your risk of heart disease and lowering blood pressure. Trans fats carry inflammation and are very harmful to our bodies. They raise your cholesterol levels (LDL). Ex: donuts, pies, margarine, cookies, and microwave popcorn. Healthy fats that improve our bodily functions: seeds, nuts, avocados, and fatty fish!

<u>MY</u> philosophy:
**Everyone doesn't need to be meatless but
you certainly need to eat meat LESS!**

WHAT IS THE BEST TIME TO EAT?

Your meal planning depends on your schedule. Eat breakfast within the first 30-60 minutes of waking up and every 3-4 hours after that. If you work a 9-5 you wont eat lunch at the same time as a person who works overnight. Your successful eating schedule is going to be unique to you. While it is recommended to eat every 3 hours it is also important to eat according to your physical activity for the day. Once you begin eating more than your body needs to perform, those foods will store as fat. You need more fuel on the days you exercise! Fuel: nutrient dense meals with carbohydrates, proteins and fats.

AM I ACTUALLY HUNGRY?

Often people tend to overeat because they are associating food with a way to meet an emotional need: stress, boredom, loneliness, or excitement. Real hunger is physical. Real hunger will make you feel a growl in your stomach, irritable and even cause a slight headache. As a baby you ate when you were hungry and if you weren't hungry you repelled the bottle. As adults we have grown accustomed to use food as entertainment, comfort or to keep busy. So the next time you're hungry check for physical signs in your body and drink a glass of water first. Sometimes you aren't hungry you are dehydrated.

PORTION CONTROL:

Protein: the palm of your hand (3.5-4oz)
Nuts/seeds: handful (1/4 cup)
Veggies: 2 handfuls (1-2 cups)
Oils/nut butters: size of your thumb (1 oz)

Carbs: your cupped hand

WATER:

You need to drink half of your body weight in ounces of water daily!

Detox water: ¼ cup mint leaf, ½ sliced cucumber, ½ sliced lemon, 2 tbsp Apple cider vinegar

Morning cleanse: 12 ounces luke warm water, ½ inch knob grated ginger (or pinch of cayenne pepper), juice of ½ lemon

FOODS THAT FIGHT INFLAMMATION:

Beets, Tomatoes, Pomegranate, Blueberries, Kale, Pineapple, Ginger, Garlic, Turmeric

FOODS THAT ELIMINATE MUCUS:

Cucumbers, Citrus fruits, celery, radishes, asparagus, Brussels sprouts

FOODS THAT BOOST ENERGY:

Apples, Oranges, Spinach, Kiwi, Sweet potatoes

EXERCISE

HOW MUCH CARDIO DO I NEED?

Adults need 150 minutes of moderate aerobic activity per week: brisk walking, biking, swimming or yard work.

OR adults can opt to participate in 75 minutes of higher intensity cardio: stair master, running, HIIT cardio.

Cardio increases blood circulation and is vital to your heart health. Don't skip it!

DO I REALLY NEED TO STRENGTH TRAIN?

Yes! As we age our bodies lose muscle mass and that increases our risk of falling and getting injured. Strength training minimum twice per week hitting major muscle groups along with moderate cardio is a baseline for general health! Strength training can include resistance bands, dumbbells, kettle bells, barbells, machines, etc.

Body weight exercises (resistance training) can improve your strength! Once you can lift your own body weight (push ups, squats, lunges, etc.) you should add weights to maximize your efforts!

IMPORTANT NOTE:

If you LOVE dancing and can do it consistently per week to meet your general health requirements then by all means DANCE! That goes for Pilates or yoga as well. It is important to not lose too much muscle mass, core strength or cardiovascular endurance. The workouts provided in this program are workouts that I personally do and love. There is no one size fits all workout plan. I eat and workout according to my goals. I encourage you to do the same! Beginners: feel free to take longer breaks and complete fewer rounds as you build up!

RECIPES

BREAKFAST RECIPES:

ASPARAGUS QUICHE

6 servings

YOU NEED:

2½ cups sliced asparagus

4 egg whites

2 whole eggs

⅓ cup diced red onion

1½ cups cooked spinach

½ cup cherry tomatoes cut in half or diced tomatoes

Light salt, pepper, Mrs. Dash table blend to taste.

HOW:

Preheat oven 350. When cutting asparagus make sure to remove the tough stems from the bottom before adding the sliced tips and spears into the mixture. Combine all ingredients into a mixing bowl the pour into a 9-inch pie dish or quiche bowl. Bake at 350 for about 45 minutes, top with grated parmesan cheese. Enjoy for brunch! Less than 35 calories a slice!

OATS

1 serving

YOU NEED:
½ cup steel cut oats
½ cup Unsweetened almond or cashew milk
1 tsp cinnamon
1 cup sliced fresh strawberries

HOW:
Cook oats as directed then mix in milk and cinnamon. Top with strawberries. Enjoy

CHOCOLATE DREAM SMOOTHIE

1 serving

YOU NEED:
1 cup unsweetened almond milk
2 tablespoons creamy peanut butter
1 ripe banana
1 tablespoon ground flaxseed
½ cup Greek yogurt (plain or vanilla)

HOW:
Wash ingredients. Blend in a blender until smooth.Enjoy immediately.

OVERNIGHT OATS

YOU NEED:
1 banana, ¼ cup peanut butter, 1 cup steel cut oats, 1 cup unsweetened almond milk, 1 tbsp. chia seeds, ½ tsp cinnamon, 1 tsp agave nectar

HOW:
In bowl mash banana. Add remaining ingredients to bowl and mix until well combined
Pour into airtight jar. Refrigerate for at least 3 hours. When ready to eat, stir well.

BERRY SUPERFOOD BLAST SMOOTHIE

1 serving

YOU NEED:
1 cup of water
½ cup strawberries
¼ cup blueberries
¼ cup Goji berries
1 tsp. Maca Powder
1 tsp. Chia Seeds
1 cup of Spinach

HOW:
Blend in a blender until smooth. Enjoy immediately.

POWER SKILLET

YOU NEED:

2 strips turkey bacon

2 Tbsp. olive oil

1 sweet potato, peeled & cubed in ¼ inch pieces

¼ onion, diced in ½ inch pieces

1 clove of garlic

¼ tsp ground cumin

Pink Salt and pepper to taste

4 Eggs (make 2 eggs per serving. Save half the hash for next day)

HOW:

In a sauté pan over medium-high heat, add turkey bacon and olive oil. When the turkey bacon sizzles, add sweet potatoes and spread out as much as possible to allow the potatoes to rest in the pan in 1 layer. Cook for about 5 minutes or until potatoes start to brown. Toss potatoes until all sides of potatoes are browned and turkey bacon is crisp. (about 3-5 min) While potatoes are cooking, in a separate pan, cook 2-4 eggs to your liking. Add onions, garlic, cumin, and season with salt and pepper. Allowing everything to sit in the heat of the pan for a minute or 2. Once the eggs are done, add them onto the top of the skillet or on the side. Enjoy!

LUNCH RECIPES:

SHREDDED CHICKEN

YOU NEED:
1 pound chicken breasts
1 green bell pepper chopped
1 red bell pepper chopped
½ medium yellow onion chopped 1 cup chicken stock
1 tsp pepper
¼ tsp salt
½ tsp garlic powder
½ tsp ground cumin
½ tsp cayenne pepper
1 tsp italian seasoning

HOW:
Place vegetables in slow cooker place chicken on top of vegetables add seasonings. Add 1 cup chicken stock and tomatoes cook on low for 7 hours once complete chicken should fall apart very easily and you can use a fork to "shred it"

QUINOA N' VEGGIES

YOU NEED:

¾ cup quinoa rinsed

½ teaspoon salt, divided

1 tablespoon vegetable oil

1 small carrot thinly sliced

1 medium red bell pepper, cored, seeded and chopped

2 teaspoons grated ginger

1 clove garlic sliced

2 cups snow peas trimmed

¼ teaspoon black pepper

1 egg beaten

2 scallions chopped

½ cup cilantro chopped

1 tablespoon low sodium soy sauce

HOW:

Place quinoa in a small saucepan with ¾ cup water and ¼ teaspoon salt. Bring to a boil, then reduce heat to low. Cover and cook, undisturbed, until quinoa absorbs water, about 15 minutes. Remove from heat, fluff with a fork and leave uncovered. Heat oil in a large skillet over medium-high heat. Cook carrot, stirring occasionally, until it softens, about 1 minute. Add bell pepper, ginger, garlic, if desired; cook, stirring frequently, about 2 minutes. Add peas, sprinkle with remaining ¼ teaspoon salt and pepper and cook, stirring frequently, 1 minute. Remove vegetables and return skillet to heat; add quinoa, along with egg. Cook, stirring constantly, until egg is evenly distributed, about 2 minutes. Add vegetables, scallions, cilantro and soy sauce; cook 1 minute more. Divide stir-fry among 4 bowls; serve warm

EZEKIEL N TUNA

YOU NEED:
half can of tuna
Ezekiel bread
2 tsp of avocado
2 tsp mustard
1 boiled egg.

HOW:
Place tuna, 2 tsp mustard and 1 chopped boiled egg white into a small bowl and mix with your hands to form small patty. Lightly toast one slice of Ezekiel bread, spread 2 tsp of avocado on top and add the tuna on top. Enjoy!

TUNA STUFFED AVOCADO:

YOU NEED:
6 avocados
6 cans of tuna in water (albacore)
1 diced red pepper
1 finely chopped jalapeño
1 cup finely chopped cilantro,
2 squeezed limes,
3 tbsp mustard
3 boiled egg whites finely chopped
1 tsp cayenne pepper

HOW:
Remove the pit of the avocado and Scoop out some of each avocado to widen the space for the tuna. Take that extra avocado and place

in a bowl & mash with fork. Add the drained tuna, cilantro, cayenne pepper, lime, jalapeño, mustard & egg whites to the bowl and mix very well then scoop the tuna into the avocado bowls. Season with light salt & pepper!

GARDEN STEW

4 servings

YOU NEED:
1 red bell pepper
3 small zucchini chopped
2 cups of green beans (cut ends)
1 tbsp parsley
¼ cup vegetable or chicken broth
1 tbsp basil
1 chopped onion
2 cloves of garlic
½ tsp cayenne pepper
1 cup chopped tomatoes
1 small can tomato sauce
1 tsp black pepper
1 tsp sea salt

HOW:
Place the garlic, onion, pepper and broth in a large pot on the stove. Cook until it starts to soften, about 4–5 minutes. Then add the chopped zucchini, cut green beans, tomatoes and tomato sauce. Add in seasonings and herbs. Heat and let simmer for 20 minutes.
Separate into 4 equal servings. Enjoy :)

SUPERFOOD SALAD

2 servings

YOU NEED:
You need:
4 cups Spinach
2 cups thinly sliced cucumbers
2 cups thinly sliced strawberries
⅓ cup feta cheese
¼ cup Unsalted sunflower seeds
4 boiled eggs chopped

HOW:
Clean Spinach thoroughly. Finely chop the veggies. Boil the eggs. In a large bowl add all ingredients and toss well. Squeeze Lemon or balsamic vinaigrette for dressing! Split salad in half into two bowls for proper portion control.
Enjoy.

DINNER RECIPES

ZESTY COD!

YOU NEED:
5 oz cod filet
1 teaspoon turmeric
½ teaspoon freshly grated ginger
2 table spoons fresh squeezed lemon juice
½ cup fresh squeezed orange juice
½ oz fresh squeezed lime
½ chopped garlic clove
2 ½ tbsp. extra virgin olive oil
black pepper
asparagus spears (6)

HOW:
(Preheat oven to 350 for veggies) Combine, lemon juice, lime-juice, orange juice, garlic and ginger in a bowl. Add the EVOO to a skillet over medium heat. Place 6 asparagus spears in the oven with lemon slices. Place the fish in the skillet and cook for 3 to 4 minutes per side, or until golden and just cooked all the way through. Please do not consume raw fish. Remove the fish and set aside. Take the contents of the bowl and pour into the skillet, bring the heat up higher for about 2 minutes. Add lemon to taste if necessary and keep stirring. Place the fish into the skillet again and coat with sauce, remove after 2 minutes. Let asparagus cool and ENJOY!

STUFFED BELL PEPPERS

YOU NEED:

4-6 large green bell peppers

1 lb ground turkey

2 tbsp. olive oil

1 cup fresh baby spinach

¼ cup tomato sauce

1 ½ cups cooked brown rice

14 oz. diced tomatoes fresh or canned (drain)

½ cup of shredded low fat cheddar cheese

1 Tbsp grated parmesan cheese

1 tsp Mrs. Dash fiesta lime

1 ½ tsp garlic powder

1 tsp pepper

3 Tbsp Italian seasoning

HOW:

Preheat oven to 350. Prepare skillet with olive oil. Cut the bell peppers in half width wise and remove all seeds. Bake peppers for approx. 12-17 minutes. Over medium heat, add onion, garlic clove, and spinach to the skillet. Saute a minute or two then brown the ground turkey and season with Mrs. Dash, Italian seasoning, light salt and pepper. Cook completely, if necessary drain excess from skillet. Add ¼ cup of tomato sauce mix well on low heat for 5 minutes. Combine cooked brown rice together with turkey mixture. Spoon into each pepper half and fill entirely. Sprinkle cheese and bake for 5 minutes

BURRITO BOWL

2 servings

YOU NEED:
1 cup brown rice
1 bunch kale chopped finely
1 avocado
2 cups black beans
2 tbsp cilantro
2 Tbsp olive oil
Sauce ingredients:
Juice of 1 lime
¼ tsp sea salt
½ tsp pepper
red pepper flakes (optional)
cayenne pepper (optional)

HOW:
Cook brown rice, add pinch of sea salt, juice of ½ lime and 2 tbsp chopped cilantro then set aside. Thoroughly clean and finely chop kale. In a large bowl whisk together 1 tbsp olive oil, pinch of cayenne pepper, salt and the juice from the other half of the lime! Toss well. Remove the pit from the avocado and slice thin. Heat the black beans and add a dash of cayenne pepper. Serve in a bowl chipotle style or spoon brown rice on the left, black beans on the right, kale in the middle and avocado to garnish. Distribute the 2 servings evenly.

BAKED SALMON & ASPARAGUS

YOU NEED:
(2) 6oz skinless salmon filets
1 lb bundle of asparagus
2 ½ tbsp. of olive oil
2 ½ tbsp. of garlic powder
Mrs. Dash lemon pepper
1 lemon slice it thin
parsley.

HOW:
Preheat oven to 400.
Cut 4 sheets of aluminum foil. Divide asparagus about 6 spears onto each sheet of foil. Rub spears with EVOO and lightly sprinkle w/salt & pepper. Clean fish, sprinkle salt & pepper and mrs dash lemon pepper. Place fish on asparagus and place 2 thin slices of lemon and parsley on top and fold the foil over to cover. Bake for about 35-30 minutes until fish is thoroughly cooked. Each is 1 serving. Enjoy!

KALE SALAD

YOU NEED:
2 servings ingredients:
2 bunches of kale
2 cups of brown lentils
½ cup dried cranberries
3 tbsp olive oil
½ cup lemon juice
3-4 tbsp olive oil
1 tsp black pepper
¼ cup pecans
½ tsp sea salt
2 cloves of garlic

HOW:
Remove stems & Clean kale thoroughly in a deep bowl with cold water!
Finely chop the greens. Begin cooking the brown lentils as directed
on packaging. In a medium saucepan add 1.5 tbsp olive oil and garlic
cloves. after about 2 minutes or so add 2 cups of kale at a time. stirring
frequently. as it wilts toss in lemon juice. When kale is done place
in a large bowl and cover. Add in cooked lentils and garnish with
dried cranberries and pecans :) Squeeze Lemon for dressing! Enjoy.

CHICKEN KABOBS

YOU NEED:
1.5 lb skinless chicken breast
1 pineapple
1 red onion
1 tbsp olive oil
½ tsp pepper
½ tsp garlic powder
1 green bell pepper
1 tsp turmeric
½ cup lemon juice
¼ tsp sea salt
1 lime
½ cup cilantro

HOW:
Cut chicken into 2 inch cubes. Combine dry seasonings & olive oil in a bowl and whisk then add chicken and marinate in the fridge for 1-2 hours. Cut the pineapple in 2 inch cubes. cut red onion and green pepper about 1 inch long and wide.
Preheat oven to 350.
Place chicken, pineapple, onion then pepper on skewer alternating the pieces. place parchment paper on a baking sheet. add skewers to baking sheet and bake for about 20 minutes
Cook brown rice separately. Finely chop cilantro and squeeze the juice of 1 lime into the cooked rice.. Mix this well! Serve 2 chicken skewers over cilantro lime rice.

SNACK RECIPES

STRAWBERRY & SPINACH SALAD

YOU NEED:

1 ½ cups spinach

1 cup strawberries

1 medium apple diced

2 tbsp sliced almonds

juice of 1 lemon

1 tbsp ACV

1 tbsp olive oil.

HOW:

mix well in a bowl and enjoy!

WATERMELON & CUCUMBER SALAD

YOU NEED:

3 cups of fresh watermelon cut into 1 inch cubes

3 cucumbers cut into quarter slices

1 tbsp olive oil

½ tsp sea salt

¼ cup crumbled feta cheese.

HOW:

Add all ingredients in a bowl and toss well.

ENERGY BITES

4 servings

YOU NEED:
1 ripe banana
¼ cup raw almonds
1 tbsp chia seeds
1 cup oats
pinch of vanilla
2 pitted dates

HOW:
Using a fork, mash your banana well.
In a food processor or blender, add the almonds
and pulse until they
are ground. Afterwards add the chia seeds and oats
then pulse again. Finally, add the banana, dates and vanilla. Blend it
until it's a thick paste texture. With clean, slightly wet, hands scoop
up the mixture and form small balls. Place them on a serving dish
separated evenly. Cover and place in the fridge.

KALE CHIPS

YOU NEED:

3-4 huge handfuls of Kale, rinsed & DRY (purple if you can find it!)
1 Tbs. Extra Virgin Olive Oil
1 clove minced garlic (optional)
Pinch of Sea Salt

HOW:

Preheat oven to 350°

In a small bowl, gently stir the minced garlic with the olive oil. Set aside to infuse. Tear off "chip size" pieces of Kale from the stem and put them into a large bowl.

Drizzle oil mixture over the kale and toss thoroughly until every "chip" is coated lightly. Spread leaves out on 1-2 baking sheets and sprinkle lightly with sea salt. Bake for about 18-20 minutes or until Kale has reached your favorite "chip like" consistency!

HEALTHY SWAPS

Spaghetti - Spaghetti squash, zucchini/beet/sweet potato noodles

Chips - Baked sweet potato chips or beet chips or kale chips

Fries - Baked sweet potato fries

Rice - Cauliflower rice

Mashed potatoes - Mashed rutabaga

Pizza Crust - Crust made with cauliflower rice

Baking with flour - Almond flour or coconut flour

Salt - lemon juice (salad dressing, fish, chicken, etc.)

Milk/dairy - Almond milk or coconut milk

Potatoes at breakfast - Sliced tomatoes

Sandwich bread - Lettuce wrap

Mayonnaise - Honey mustard

Sugar - Coconut sugar, honey, or stevia

Sour cream - Greek yogurt, coconut oil

Toast - Ezekiel or sprouted bread

Croutons - Sliced almonds (in salad)

Bowl of ice cream - Small Bowl of frozen cherries or grapes

I'm proud of your dedication to this 30-day quest. I pray that this journey encourages you to not count calories but to count blessings! The body you have now is a visual manifestation of the decisions you've made in the past. So the decisions you make from here on out will determine the body will have in the future. Cheers to many healthy and fit years!

With light & love,
Coach Caprice

IG: @CoachCaprice

Here is Caprice's testimony, which has motivated many clients to date:

In 2007, Caprice survived a serious car accident, leaving her with a Traumatic Brain Injury, unable to walk and impaired cognitive abilities—to the point where she had difficulty following simple instructions. Thanks to the help of an extensive 5-month regimen of physical, speech and occupational therapy, Caprice recovered and reunited with her friends at school. There, she joined her high school track team and quickly rose to stardom, winning every race and was named conference champion in all of her events. While she had to adjust to high school, Caprice moved forward excuse free, not stopping herself from doing what she loved!

After getting back on her feet and returning to a 'normal' life, Caprice was unfortunately in another car accident, just three years later. She was left with Tonic-clonic seizures, which became a lifelong pattern that would later be diagnosed as Epilepsy. In fact, in 2012 she suffered a prolonged seizure after hitting her head that caused retrograde amnesia, leaving her with no memory of the first nineteen years of her life. Caprice woke up in a hospital, not knowing her name or the family that surrounded her. She was admitted into every major research and top-notch hospital in the country (Mayo Clinic, Christ, Loyola, Northwestern, UIC, etc.), until she received the Epilepsy diagnosis.

While all of this could have brought anyone down, Caprice was fueled by her battle and decided to 'stomp out every excuse'. In her eyes, there was no excuse to not stay healthy and fit, as it always made her feel better, empowering her to focus her energy on what she could do, instead of being tied down by her circumstances. It made her feel unbreakable.

Depression led her dad to take her to the gym with him. After falling in love with fitness and climbing out, Caprice became certified and opened the impactful Excuse Free Fitness in Homewood, IL in 2015. With her gym, Caprice strives to provide her clients and members with a sense of hope and inspiration to never give up, *no matter* life's circumstances.

November 1st, 2018 Caprice had multiple tonic-clonic seizures, was sent to the hospital and kept for observation. November 2nd she had another seizure in the MRI scan, stopped breathing and went into respiratory arrest. She was resuscitated, intubated and placed into a medically induced coma. After 5 weeks in the hospital and 12 weeks of intensive day rehabilitation she has regained physical strength all while her spiritual and mental strength remains. She believes that even when you fall it is your choice to rise back up. Because if you can look up, you can get up! As long as you survive you have a purpose to fulfill.

Excuse Free Fitness has been thriving for almost 4 years, yet Caprice found that it was **so much more than physical pounds** that people needed to get rid of so 'Prayers Up, Weight Down' was born. She is eager to help as many people across the world as possible release physical, emotional and spiritual pounds!